So *Great* a Cloud

Journeys of *Faith* and *Courage* in South Asia

*Wherefore, seeing we also are
compassed about with
so great a cloud
of witnesses, let us...*
Hebrews 12:1

Kenneth G. Old

Foreword by Dr. Bob Paul

Tate Publishing, LLC

"So Great a Cloud" by Kenneth Old
Copyright © 2005 by Kenneth Old. All rights reserved.

Published in the United States of America
by Tate Publishing, LLC
127 East Trade Center Terrace
Mustang, OK 73064
(888) 361–9473

Book design copyright © 2005 by Tate Publishing, LLC. All rights reserved.

No part of this publication may be reproduced, stored in a retrieval system or transmitted in any way by any means, electronic, mechanical, photocopy, recording or otherwise without the prior permission of the author except as provided by USA copyright law.

Scripture quotations are taken from the *Holy Bible, King James Version,* Cambridge, 1769.

ISBN: 1–5988616–9-7

Bhajna Paul Nasarali John Samuel Lahnu Sabur Masih Mr Bakhish
    Mr Mukarji   Basso   Ramdei   Kanaya
              Hamid-ul-Din

*Dedicated to
the memory of
the courageous men
and women
whose stories are told
in the following pages*

Poetry excerpts are from *Footprints in the Dust* by Kenneth G. Old.

The more recent stories told in this book are as true as fallible memory permits. Where possible and appropriate, they have been checked with individuals involved in them. Names of people and places have sometimes been changed, and immaterial details of the stories themselves have also sometimes been altered.

Royalties from the sale of this book will be used for the education of poor Punjabi children in Pakistan.

Tales Gathered in Pakistan
1850 - 1990

Concurrence ?

*Men will die (and kill) for the truth
And for nothing more readily
So the devil's task is simply
The same as God's,
To persuade men that
What they believe
Is the truth –*

Contents

Map of Central Asia 10
Map of Pakistan 11
Foreword. 13
Dusty Road 17
Preface. 19
Introduction. 21
Certainties. 25
Elisha's Brother George 27
George Scott in Afghanistan. 31
George Before the Amir 33
George and Habibullah 35
The Megs of Jhandran. 39
Pipo 43
Long Walks for Bhajna 49
Kanaya and Ramdei 55
Ramdei in Kashmir 59
Kanaya in Kashmir 63
The Hindu Judge in Jammu 67
Kanaya Makes his Defense. 71
Kanaya: If at First You Don't Succeed… 75
Kanaya: The Hukm. 79
War or Peace 83
Ramdei at the Jammu Kutchery 87
Sabbath at the Kutchery 91
The Pandit's Night Visitors. 95
Kanaya in Jandi. 99
Bhajna & Gulabi 103
Ditt and Shahabdeke 109
Ditt the Christian. 115
Mohammed Alim 121
Chandu Ray and the Tibetan Lama. 127
Esther at the Orphanage 133
Esther at Gujranwala. 141
Esther at Chichawatni 143
The Blind Afghan 147

Dr. Razzaq and the Qadianis............................151
Gulsher 157
Kalim - Outward Journey 161
Kalim - Homecoming...............................167
Sadiq Shamshad 171
Mementos 177
Epilogue 179
Appendix: Urdu Dictionary 181

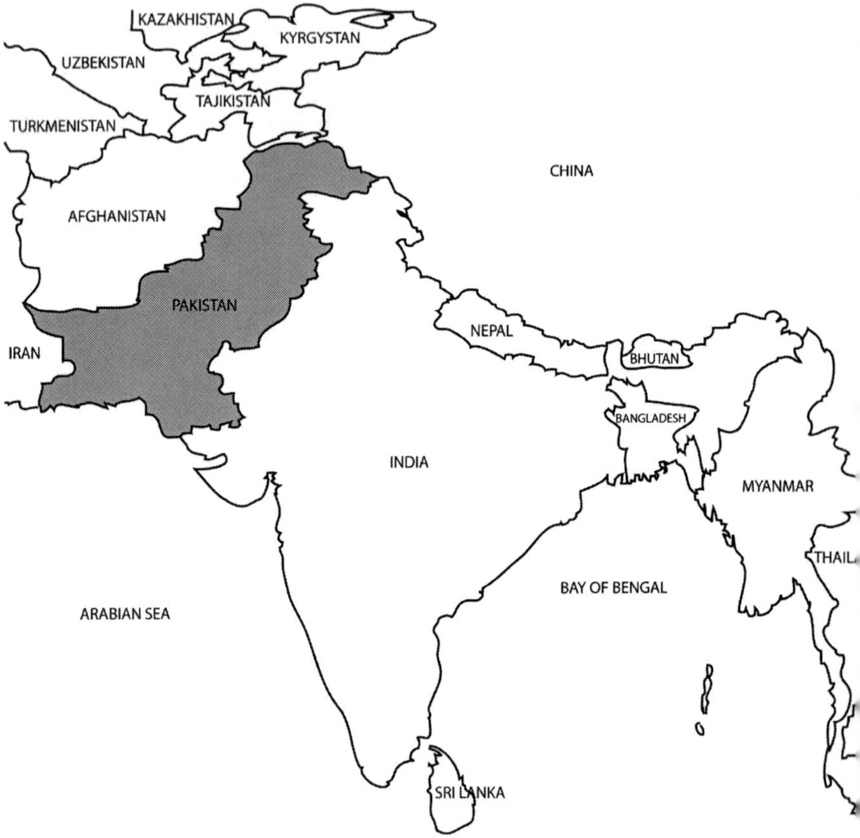
KAZAKHISTAN
KYRGYSTAN
UZBEKISTAN
TAJIKISTAN
TURKMENISTAN
CHINA
AFGHANISTAN
PAKISTAN
NEPAL
IRAN
BHUTAN
BANGLADESH
INDIA
MYANMAR
THAIL
BAY OF BENGAL
ARABIAN SEA
SRI LANKA

UZBEKISTAN
TAJIKISTAN
TURKMENISTAN
CHINA
Gilgit
Skardu
Peshawar
Kabul
Taxila
Rawalpindi
KASHMIR
AFGHANISTAN
Jhelum
Jammu
Sialkot
Zafarwal
Gujranwala
Lahore
PAKISTAN
New Delhi
IRAN
INDIA
Hyderabad
Karachi
ARABIAN SEA

Foreword

This modest volume contains diamonds. Brilliant, pure light flashes from the rare gems of Christian character whose stories are told here. Their witness, formed of simple human material and forged under extreme pressure, proves that 'our extremity is God's opportunity to display his glory', as Anne Dutton said. They also remind us that the Lord has no regard for those things that we are tempted to think make for greatness.

Ken Old's friends have long delighted in his remarkable gifts as a raconteur and poet. This little book will be treasured as part of that legacy, along with his earlier volumes of poetry and the recently published larger account of his experiences in Pakistan, *Walking the Way*. The reader who comes into possession of this present volume first should by all means obtain a copy of the former. The two books, along with his collections of poems, are deeply complementary.

This book is fashioned of extra material that did not quite fit the earlier volume, but which was simply too good to leave untold. What has been assembled here is more, however, than merely a collection of leftovers. As a missionary friend suggested to Ken, these stories should be of value in the first place to the Punjabi church, for their historical interest and spiritual example. Secondly, their retelling under Ken's deft hand preserves in part Andrew Gordon's history of the first thirty years of the Sialkot Mission, an old book long out of print and not easily found. This is an important resource for research and study of the broader historical legacy of Christian missions.

I would suggest that these stories also hold considerable contemporary value for the wider body of Christian churches, for at least two reasons. First, they exemplify history as told 'from the underside', wherein people who were regarded in their own time as being of little account emerge clearly as principal agents in advancing the Gospel. As they take their place as true heroes of the faith alongside the intrepid missionaries who also sacrificed much, but whose stories have more often been told, these witnesses and martyrs remind us that God's ways are not our ways, and so teach us humility about our grand schemes and visions. Second, to read of believers such as George Scott, Kanaya, and Esther is like reading the Book of Acts. These relatively recent apostles will encourage and challenge all those who bear the name of Christ to remember that God still works miracles, particularly for those who place their total trust in Him.

One hopes that people who are not Christians might also find the opportunity to read what Ken Old has written. His greater themes are inter-religious conflict, prejudice, injustice, and the possibilities of human beings living peaceably together despite different beliefs. Ken is nothing if not honest. As such, he is a trustworthy arbiter who never flinches from the awful truth, even when it concerns his fellow Christians, nor does he withhold praise for true goodness wherever it may be found. In an era of violent conflicts among Hindus, Muslims and Christians—not to mention secularists West and East—we need every voice that calls us to consider the common human quest for God, the true nature of righteousness, and the all-too-common human propensity to descend into bestiality (against which religion *per se* seems to have little effect). There is wisdom in this book that deserves a wide reading.

That wisdom arises from practical experience, from keen powers as an observer of human nature, from Ken's own journey as a seeker and follower of Christ. I think it comes, also, from a certain pleasure he takes in challenging conventional thinking—at least it seems so to me. I well-remember, for example, the elfish gleam in Ken's eye when he would tell my young sons that they should by no means allow their schoolwork (or their parents!) to interfere with the imaginative enterprises that were proper to being boys. What fun to meet a grownup who encouraged them to be children! Of course, he was right to do so, since they were indeed children. As time went by, the stories they heard from Ken as children, teenagers, and as young adults registered deeply. Ken remains a major influence in their desire to follow the Way of Christ, and so also for me. I have no doubt that all who read these stories, and Ken's reflections, will likewise be encouraged to consider the blessings, and count the costs, of giving their lives to the Lord Jesus Christ.

One thing remains to be said. This book, and the one that preceded it, are testimonies to the power of love. Ken started writing, I believe, out of his love for Marie, after her death. She was of course his first wife, companion and partner throughout their many years of work in Pakistan. What he wrote became more organized, and he persisted in the task, because of the indispensable help and love of Patty, his second American wife and partner. It was a privilege and joy to me, as Senior Pastor of West Side Church in Richland, Washington, to know Ken and Marie, and also Patty, to enjoy their friendship and hospitality in Richland, and also at their home in Kent. What I came to understand over time is that there was another love in Ken's life—shared and approved by Marie and Patty both. That love is for the children of Pakistan, particularly those of the Punjab, the current heirs of the same impoverished beginnings as the men and women whose stories are told in this book. The royalties that may be earned from sales of this book will go to them—for their education, for their future, for their opportunities to discover the God whose love is beyond all imagining, and who cherishes them infinitely.

I once heard Ken say that if love is not at the heart of what we are doing, we should not do it. In writing and publishing this small, but superb book, which will benefit the children he loves so dearly, Ken has followed his own counsel. For that, many will be blessed.

Dr. Bob Paul
Senior Pastor, West Side Church (1985–2005)
President, Medical Ambassadors International

Dusty Road

And so, O Man, I took you at your word –
You said to knock and sure I would be heard,
You said to seek and sure I'd be to find
The kingdom's door though mine eye be blind,
You said to ask and sure I'd be to get
Well, Man, I've knocked, I've sought, I've asked –
– and yet!
Then next, O Man, I took you at your word –
For my very troubled soul (O Lord)
You said to come and surely I'd have rest
You said to trust like any child would trust
And such a faith could move the highest hill –
Well, Man, I've trusted like a child –
– and still!
And so, O Man, I took you at your word
Once more. Do you remember what you said?
Except a man deny upon the rack
Himself and put a cross upon his back
Instead and follow where you first had trod –
Well, Man, I've got the load –
– so help me, God!
And now, O Man, don't get ahead, that's all –
The mist is in my eyes and I shall fall.
I don't know where or how, you know the way.
Just share the road and ever with me stay.
I'll walk, I'll stumble just where you have trod –
Trudging in your dust, Man who could be God!

Kenneth Old

Preface

During the first couple of years after my wife Marie's death from the recurrence of cancer, I spent time writing what was initially to be her biography.

Marie and I had been missionaries of the Sialkot Mission of the United Presbyterian Church of North America for much of our working lives. The land where we had worked is now the modern Pakistan.

The book(s) grew and changed during the writing under the influence of the material I was acquiring.

In addition to earlier information about Marie's life, there were scores of incidents to record from the years that we had spent together in northern Pakistan.

Interesting stories also crossed my path that were not directly relevant to the unfolding narrative. They are stories where the heroes and the heroines–yes, and the villains too–are Indians and Pakistanis or Afghans.

I had several choices about these stories. I could discard or shorten them or I could give them the justice I felt they merited by a lengthier treatment in a different setting. A number of them, refreshingly and poignantly courageous, related to the beginnings of the mission to which we were affiliated.

A remark by a fellow missionary indicating that some of the tales would be of historical value to the Punjabi church persuaded me to separate them and some later stories into this present volume.

They give examples of the human character pushed to extremity. Again and again they demonstrate the strength and weakness of the simple human soul and its immense qualities of courage, tenacity, love and faith.

The source for the early stories is a little known history of the first thirty years of the Sialkot Mission–"Our India Mission"– written by its founder, Andrew Gordon. The book is out of print. This mission, which had an effective life of about one hundred years, was founded just prior to the Indian Mutiny, as it is known in the West, of 1857.

In the stories that follow, the words "Yisu" and "Isa" for Jesus have been used interchangeably.

These are a small random collection of wild flowers, by no means a full bouquet, gathered from India, from Kashmir, from Pakistan and from Afghanistan. Somewhere in each story we meet qualities of character we would desire in ourselves, and we meet faith and faithfulness to an exceptional degree.

Summer 2005
Kenneth Old
Sellindge, Kent
England

Introduction

*Wherefore, seeing we also are compassed about
with so great a cloud of witnesses,
let us lay aside every weight, and the sin which doth so easily beset us,
and let us run with patience the race that is set before
us, looking unto Jesus . . . Hebrews 12:1*

As we grow into adulthood, we become successively wrapped in accruing mantles of relationships, interests, attractions and distractions. The simplicity of our childhood days becomes blurred and lost in the complexities of coping with life and its confusions. The earlier certainties become hesitations and questions, and then deeper questionings. We are no longer as sure as we were. Doubts assail us. We dare to wonder how soundly the certainties of our fathers were based on fact or truth, or whether it is possible they could have been misled or mistaken. We even question our own culture and measure it against others.

We are growing up, and doubt and resolution are an essential part of that journey. To most of us they inform and mold our characters and conduct. They are not in essence life threatening.

*God incites us to rebel
Against the well regarded
And the comfortable,
Against the certainties
And suppositions of our time
And the clichés
That point to Him
Throwing us instead,
Stripped bare,
Upon some wave lashed rock
With barely a toehold
To be slashed by the spume
And know our helplessness*

Kenneth Old

Some of these stories that follow have a more somber import. A dozen men and women rooted in the culture of the Indian subcontinent and Afghanistan, daring to rethink who they are, and often meeting with immense courage the consequences of diverging from the familiar.

The very essence of the Christian faith is its individuality. At some later point, the call to fellowship unites disparate human beings in a common exuberance of praise and worship.

Before this however, God is working in a different way. He is gathering grains of sand from the seashores of His world and dealing with each one separately, as though nothing else exists except the single grain and the Hand that holds it. Sometimes swiftly, sometimes slowly, the certainties are being stripped away. It is an essential prelude for what is to follow. He already knows the consequences. This is the preparation to equip them who would choose and follow a different Way for what will happen.

Blind, frozen by the driven snow,
Naked, back to the wall, while
The circle of wolves closes in
And the first leap cleaves the air –

The one prelude to forgiveness
And the loneliness of His life.

The loneliness of His life is the essential identification. It is the most significant person-to-person encounter they will ever have, a strange mystical merging of two identities where the normal primary instinct of self-preservation becomes submerged in a more determined resolution to be true to Him at all costs.

For most of them it will cost all their prior securities. They will lose their support communities and their work opportunities. Their friends and neighbors will oppose them bitterly; their families will line up with the others and join in the shouts of anger, disgust and derision.

Let none of us who stand secure at lesser cost deride those who face the helplessness and are broken by it. We have no right to judge them, but only to wonder how far we might have journeyed in their shoes.

Be encouraged!

Certainties

With footsteps firm
We stride along
Among a host of brothers
Savoring certainties
Acquired from our fathers.
We shout the questions down
That threaten our perceptions,
Sharply still the voices
That hint of other choices.
Thus zealots are born
And martyrs created.

Elisha's Brother George

1855

Elisha Swift is an Indian boy growing up in Ludhiana Mission Orphanage in the Punjab of India. He is given a new name by the administrator. It is recognition of a supporting American donor.

Elisha initially meets Andrew Gordon while Andrew is building the first mission bungalow of the Sialkot Mission at Hajipura in 1855/56.

Elisha and a colleague, both Christian catechists from a neighboring mission based in Lahore, are itinerating on an evangelistic tour near Sialkot when their tent is looted by robbers. This leads to their meeting with Gordon, a new young missionary from a Presbyterian church in the United States who is working nearby.

He finds their fluent English, their obvious integrity and their acumen in dealing with his own particular robbers–rascally workmen, suppliers and supervisors 'cooking' the building bills–a great help. They stay a couple of days to help him sort things out.

Over a meal and then on into the evening, by light of a vegetable oil lamp hung from a tent post, Elisha tells the story of his younger brother, George. George Scott too has been named after a donor to the orphanage in which they and one other brother, Daniel, have grown up. An older brother has earlier joined the British army in India and gone into Afghanistan with the troops. He is to die there. Another brother, Harbhajan, accompanies him and returns safely.

In the mission the three boys acquire good English fluency. This is sure to be helpful to them when they begin searching for jobs. At the orphanage the three Hindu boys become Christian.

George eventually, like Elisha before him, leaves the orphanage to try to make his way in the world.

He has no job and is soon completely destitute. He is alone in the jungle. He has nothing in sight for his next meal. In a desperate prayer he turns his life over to God to do with it as He wills. It is the essential change-point in his life. His commitment never falters from this time forward.

An early photo has been preserved of George and shows a young, determined man with deep-set eyes and full lips, bearded with a full frizzy beard and wearing the loosely wrapped puggree turban of the ordinary Punjabi villager.

He moves on to Peshawar and finds work as a clerk in a grocery and household supplies store. Nabi Baksh is one of those Indian supply contractors whose business is founded on supplying the British garrisons and their families in cantonments across the country. They import an incredible variety of English goods produced for the colonies and dependencies in the factories of Birmingham and Bradford.

George rapidly gains the trust of Nabi Baksh, a Muslim. There is something about the young man that creates confidence. Keys, money, the business itself can be left without worry in his hands. It is almost as though it is because he is a Christian, rather than in spite of this particular regrettable religious affiliation.

The disastrous first Kabul war (1839–42) is over. It is the first major conflict of the new Queen's reign. The news and dispatches from this landlocked country, where not even a single copy of the Bible is known to exist, have stirred the whole of England. William Carey, the Baptist shoemaker from Northampton, founder of the modern missionary movement, has been long settled in India. He has stirred evangelical England with hopes, even the duty, of bringing the Gospel into the darkest corners of the empire. The cross and the missionaries to announce the gospel shall follow after the troops.

A devout and wealthy woman in England, anticipating military success in Afghanistan, sends a donation of beautifully printed and bound Bibles—in the correct language—to be distributed to the people of Kabul. Addressed c/o Colonel Wheeler, a pious Army officer, they arrive in Peshawar.

In the later history of the church in India the individual Christian influence of certain British army officers has been significant, right up until 1947. One might even say in the history of India itself.

The British Raj was, as the colonial governing power, at pains to administer with wisdom and fairness the religious interests of Hindus, Muslims, Sikhs and a multitude of other smaller sects, cults and sub groups. To do otherwise would have been setting a match to a powder keg. It was scrupulous to be evenhanded and to avoid favoring Christian interests over others. Even so, many individual administrators and officers were deeply committed to Christ in their personal faith. This commitment inevitably guided their judgments and found expression in their spare time pursuits.

Col. Wheeler's plan is not to distribute the Bibles free but to send them to Kabul for sale by some Hindu, Muslim or Jewish merchant. A camel caravan through the Khyber Pass will take them up, in the normal way by which merchandise is sent. He asks Scott to try to locate a camel caravan returning to Kabul.

His search in the bazars (markets) and caravansarais (staging point for camel caravans) draws only laughter and ridicule. "Bibles to Kabul! Are we worth nothing? Why should we die? Do we also not have children?"

He reports his failure back to Col. Wheeler but offers to leave his job and take the Bibles himself.

This takes the colonel aback. The lad is capable, enthusiastic and clearly faithful, but hardly mature enough in years to handle the risks involved. His life would be at stake were he to be discovered. He is surely too young to hazard his life in such a way. Yet God had used David when he was merely a boy! He had called Samuel when he was but a child. Could He not use this young man also?

The two agree to make the whole enterprise a matter of prayer for seven days and then to meet again. When they do, George is more clear than previously. He is to take the Bibles, and God will watch over him and bring him back safely.

The Bibles are packed in boxes, wrapped and sewn in cloth and loaded onto mules. There is a long journey ahead of two hundred miles across plains and through gorges and passes until the final climb onto the Kabul plateau. George takes some other goods from Nabi Baksh to also trade. Exotic perfumes are not bulky and attract both men and women buyers.

They pray together and then, the following dawn, the young man is on his way across the plain to Jamrud village and the mouth of the Khyber. The British are recent to the Frontier and are yet to gain control of the passes; that will take another three decades. Once off the Peshawar plain, the young man will be on his own.

George Scott In Afghanistan

1850

Only a mile into the pass, George and his mules catch up with the slow and measured pace of a caravan of camels heading back to Kabul. They are loaded with goods from the bazars of Peshawar, and with goods farther afield from the transshipment warehouses of the city.

Greetings are exchanged. George willingly accepts the invitation to travel in company. He is uneasy, however, and his trouble will not leave his mind alone. He has been greeted with a first casual question, "Who are you?" and has responded in an oblique way that could leave the impression that he too is a Muslim. Yes, that answer, given on the spur of the moment and not premeditated, has seemed to offer a security while he travels, but has not God assured him that He would be his Protector?

George increases speed to catch up with the leader of the caravan, striding alone in the middle of the long strung train of almost thirty camels.

"Malikji", he begins nervously, making sure to address him with respect. "You must not believe I am a Muslim. I am a Christian. It is Bibles I am taking to Kabul. I know I am risking my life to do so, but I started out trusting God to keep me safe. When one of your men asked me who I was, I did not reply clearly to him that I was a Christian, and I feel I denied God. I could not feel safe until I came to tell you this. You must do as you will."

The leader raises his hand in reassurance and smiles at the young man as he continues unbroken his long steady stride. "Your concerns are not mine. Do not worry yourself. You shall travel with us and we will protect you until you choose to leave us. Furthermore, do not worry at all about your meals. We will provide you with food, and you may either eat with us or by yourself as you shall choose. Have no fear. Your life is my life. Travel at ease."

In just over a week, ascending steadily, they are on the outskirts of Kabul, a mud walled mud-housed city dominated by the protruding ridge from the south where the midday gun is mounted. Below is the stone palace of Dost Mohammed, the ruling Amir (Afghan ruler), and beyond it the river winding its way through the city towards the gorge and towards India.

George takes quarters in the caravansarai where his traveling friends have chosen to stay until they dispose of the burdens they have brought and acquire others to take back down to the plains.

He wastes no time. Nabi Baksh has taught him that unsold goods represent loss of income. In order to move goods, you must display them and then actively discover buyers for them. He spreads his rugs upon the ground, brings out his boxes and other goods, and places his Bibles on display. They have attractive bindings and the lettering, in Arabic script, is tooled in gold leaf. The Q'ran Sharif (The Holy Koran) is a slimmer volume than these books are. Passers-by pause to inquire. George, his basic Pushtu (language of Pathan tribesmen) idiomized by long conversations with the camel drivers, easily finds answers. Does not the Q'ran Sharif itself acknowledge the Torah (books of Moses), the Zaburs (Psalms) and the Injil (New Testament) as the word of God? They are all to be found here in this remarkable volume.

The morning after his arrival, there has been no disturbance so far. It is reported to the Amir that there is a Christian in the Caravansarai Gulistan selling Bibles. An officer arrests George. As he is led away he asks the neighboring teashop owner to keep an eye on his goods until he can return. He does not know quite when that will be. He does not know he will not see them again.

George Before The Amir

1850

George is brought promptly before the Amir himself.

His brief answers confirm the ruler's questions. The Amir's decision is equally straightforward. "You have forfeited your life! You must die!"

There is only one way the young man before him may save his life. "If you renounce your Christian religion and repeat before me the Kalma (Muslim creed) then I will spare your life. If you will say "There is but one God and Mohammed is His Prophet," you may go back to your own country and I will give you safe conduct to get home. If you do not, you shall surely die."

George dares argue. "Sir, you allow Hindu and Jewish merchants to travel through your country and sell their goods wherever they can find buyers. You do not interfere with them but allow them free passage. I am only trying to do the same. I am not giving anything away. If your people do not like my products they do not need to buy them."

This reasoning carries no weight with Dost Mohammed.

"Say the Kalma or suffer the death penalty. There is no alternative. One or the other. That is it!"

Once again George, his life on the line, has nothing to lose by arguing.

"But, sir, if I say the Kalma with my lips and not my heart, what gain is that? First my heart has to be persuaded that what you say is the Truth, and then my lips will follow without hesitation. First convince me that your faith is right and mine wrong, and assuredly I will repeat the Kalma as you require."

The young man is throwing down a challenge. Faith to faith. Very well!

The Amir agrees. He perceives no difficulty. He will persuade this ignorant young Punjabi of the Truth. There is one among them who can do this without difficulty. He sends for Habibullah. Habibullah is brought. He is not only fluent in English, a mark of high educational standing, but also in Hindi, for he has received his education at George's own alma mater, a mission school on the plains of India. Let this worm wriggle as he may. He will not wriggle off this hook!

These two former Ludhiana students now face each other before a king in his court, hundreds of miles away in another country. The cost of failure will be for one his life and for the other, ignominy. The contest is on Habibullah's home ground; the judges believe as Habibullah does. None will dare even one Afghani coin that the young man will escape. Perhaps Col. Wheeler has not been so wrong to think in terms of David and Goliath when he sent this young man forth.

The Amir, his ministers and friends, and even the merely curious among the court hangers-on, ease themselves back to enjoy the sport. The Amir gives Habibullah his instructions.

"Persuade this young man of the errors of his faith and the truth of our own faith. He has said he will then recite the Kalma. Proceed!"

GEORGE AND HABIBULLAH

1850

All eyes are on Habibullah, defender of the faith.

"You Christians, because of terms such as 'God' used in your Bible in reference to Jesus the Prophet, conclude that he is divine. However, your own Bible also uses such terms to describe others whom you yourselves admit are merely men."

George denies such a passage exists.

"Will you recite the creed if I show you such a passage?"

"Certainly, show it to me."

Habibullah first answers with a question. "How do you spell the name of God?"

"G-O-D of course."

Habibullah reads from the 82nd Psalm. "*I have said, Ye are gods; and all of you are children of the most High. But ye shall die like men . . .*"

Placing the English Bible before his adversary, he jabs excitedly with his finger at the spot he has been reading. "There! Do you see that?"

George is taken aback by this objection to the divinity of Christ, one that he has never before heard. For a brief moment he is nonplussed, and then reminded of an eastern proverb: *An ignorant man knows not the difference between g-o-d and d-o-g.* In Persian the words for god and dog resemble each other and can confuse a poorly educated man.

His voice rings throughout the Durbar hall where the local eminences hold court. "Are you so ignorant that you do not know the difference between God and dog? Can you not see the small g?"

Laughter at the discomfiture of Habibullah ripples round the hall. This particular contest is brief, and it is already over. He is dismissed abruptly to the back of the hall.

George has acquired some stature with the court by his quick riposte although the king has by no means finished with him. He is invited, an invitation that is an implicit command, to dine with the Amir and his courtiers. In initial reaction he remarks that in India Muslims do not eat with Christians. "According to the Q'ran," comes the scornful response "it is lawful. The Muslims beyond the Indus have become little better than the people they live amongst."

George now has to decide how to give thanks before his meal. To uncover the head before the Amir would be construed as disrespect. The young man has however learned not to deviate from correct Christian conduct; God will be his Protector. He bares his head and prays. He is rebuked hotly by a courtier for daring such impoliteness before the Amir. George explains with meekness it is the custom of Christians to bare their heads before God and to give thanks to Him before a meal. His explanation is accepted as a worthwhile custom. No more is said.

The Qazi, the Muslim judge, is called to decide what shall be done with the infidel who has been selling Bibles and will not recant. The Qazi confirms the death penalty. A courtier requests the execution be postponed to allow the prisoner to think over his situation.

George is now confined to a particularly loathsome prison on the city outskirts. He becomes ill, dangerously ill. He is brought from prison, reduced to a skeleton by dysentery and fever. He can barely stand. What is the final decision? The Durbar (court) is divided. The general sentiment is to carry out the sentence without further delay.

The same courtier who previously pled for a delay in execution tries again. Why unnecessarily incur the displeasure of the British Government? The man is dying. Let him die. There is a spirited discussion whether to kill him or let him die. An old man present takes pity. "He is only a youth. He has seen little of the world. Let him live a while longer."

Finally this is agreed by all present. He is laid onto a string bed, and four men carry him. To ensure the assignment is completed and not eased by the early demise of the patient, two soldiers escort them. They carry him, weak and wasted, more than one hundred and fifty miles on their shoulders until they are in the middle of the Khyber Pass at Ali Masjid. There, friendly Afridi tribesmen promise to deliver him to the British in Jamrud and to get a receipt for him.

Col. Wheeler rejoices to see George Scott back from Kabul. He too will never know what has happened to the Bibles he received and dispatched.

With good care and medical treatment, George fully recovers and takes a teaching job in a government school. He believed until his death that although all his possessions had been taken from him in Kabul, the treasured Bibles would have been both preserved and perused, and would be the seed-sowing in Kabul that some later reaper would gather as harvest.

In 1856, in response to Andrew Gordon's invitation, he comes to Sialkot and becomes involved not only in the establishment of the Sialkot Mission as one of its first Indian workers, but also in the events that are about to occur in the village of Jhandran in the Zafarwal sub-district of Sialkot.

The Megs Of Jhandran

1957 / 1857

In November of 1957, Marie and I and a wonderful little boy of three months that we had adopted arrived in Hajipura, Sialkot. Chinese packers in Karachi, engaged by the U.S. Corps of Engineers, had relieved us of all packing concerns at the orphanage we were leaving. In a great wooden box, which we later sold to be a shop, they had packed all our worldly concerns. It arrived safely, teetering from the railway sidings on a two-wheeled bullock cart.

We lived alongside Teresa Brownlee, one of the great woman missionaries of the Sialkot Mission. Next door, at the girls' boarding school, was another, Eva Hewitt, and two younger American women, Marie and Gene.

The house where we lived was Andrew Gordon's first home in India. It was the first building of the Sialkot Mission, built over a period of six months during the winter of 1855/56. The walls of brick laid in mud were two feet thick and about seventeen feet high. The roofs were flat, covered with 12" x 6" tiles of burnt clay, and protected with 3" or more of earth, coated for waterproofing with a mud/manure/straw paste.

This house, young though it was, was full of history. It had not long been built when the 1857 Mutiny burst all around it, and the Scottish missionaries on the north side of the town were murdered while trying to get to the fort in the center of the town.

Two years later, unexpected visitors, Pipo and Fakira, came here from Jhandran with questions. In 1872 came two others from Mirali and Shahabdeke similarly unexpected–Nattu and Ditt.

Those four visitors helped give birth to a church that today is well over a million strong. So let us pause, go back a century and journey to Jhandran.

The year is 1857, the year of the Mutiny. It is autumn. The fighting is over.

From the south side of Sialkot you cross the Aik nullah (creek) by the narrow brick arch bridge. Instead of heading south for Pasrur along the narrow main road, you swing southeast for Zafarwal, twenty-six miles away. The journey is over flat, flat land. It is easy to imagine the devastation when the Aik, the Degh and the Bhed overflow. The other route via Chawinda is longer but often a better road. You ford the Degh nullah.

Three miles south of Zafarwal is a large village, Jhandran. Most of the land around the village and the larger homes within the village belong to Muslims. A few Sikhs live in the village and about twenty-five families of Megs, a low caste of Hindus who live chiefly by weaving. There are about 600,000 of this caste in the Punjab, the land of the five rivers. They also work as casual laborers in the fields and at the sugar mill on the edge of the village. Few are landowners, but two of them, Rama and Diyala, do own property and cultivable land. Their relative wealth gives them right to speak for the community as joint lambardars (headmen of the village). Rama is father of Kanaya.

The Megs are heading for a sorry religious venture.

They have been wanting a guru (Hindu religious teacher) since it is apparent that with all due respect, Fakira, one of themselves, just isn't up to it.

Now Mastan Singh has arrived. He seems to have the answers–and the qualifications they are looking for in a guru. He is from Chattiyanwala, to the south of Gujranwala district, and from a wealthy Sikh family. He is tall, young and noble-looking. He is also educated, of good talents and presentation, of easy and intelligent conversation and quite distinct religious views. He knows the way to everlasting happiness. He is given the courtesy of accommodation in the dharmsala (the community guest house), food, and a servant.

The men-folk invite him to share with them the huqqa (smoker's bubble pipe) as they squat in a comfortable and enlarging circle in the evenings. They are curious about him and indeed, he also is curious about them. "Have you people ever found God?" he asks. They shake their heads. They wait for him to answer his own question; he must have an answer.

"I am quite sure you have not, for God is not to be found in the religion of either the Muslims or the Hindus. BUT I can reveal him to you. If I shall bring him near to you so that even your very own eyes can see him, will you receive and follow me as your guru?"

He knows the custom. They will talk things over among themselves. There will be many things to consider. A guru is a charge upon a community. He also becomes their champion, their voice. The community will uphold its guru against the claims of another. There will be public discussions between rival gurus. There will be time for an answer tomorrow night.

When he is gone, the men stay and pass the long huqqa pipe-stem around the circle. Honest Pipo, a weaver, a delicate man with a grave and intelligent countenance, is so well educated that he can read. He is hesitant. They are a poor community. True, Fakira has not been very successful as their guru, but at least he is one of them, and he has been no charge upon them. Fakira, not perhaps disinterested, speaks up. The man speaks well and they all desire to see God, but can they afford an outside guru?

Rama is taken with Mastan Singh. He knows the subtleties of bargaining that they are involved in. He agrees that if they invite Mastan Singh to be their guru, he, Rama, will supply a bed, clothing, and a servant–AND daily two pounds of flour, two pounds of buffalo milk, clarified butter, salt, spices and tobacco towards his support. The whole circle of men solemnly nods approval and agreement. From now on Mastan Singh is their guru.

Mastan Singh acknowledges his appointment and the conditions imposed upon him. All in the community who wish shall be taught free of charge, and the whole community shall learn how to see God.

The new guru's method of teaching is well adapted to an audience almost entirely illiterate. They also work all day so are only available in the evenings. It is all at his tongue's end. He requires that his short lesson be memorized. Those who miss any lesson are tested the following evening anyway, so in the fields, one is rehearsing another for the evening test before the next lesson.

After a year and a half of memorizing lessons from their guru, and without one of them seeming to get anywhere near seeing God, they encourage him with some firmness to accelerate the process.

He summarizes his five conclusions:

Kenneth Old

1. We have no spirits.
2. The four elements–fire, air, earth and water–of which our bodies are composed, will return to those elements when we die.
3. There are no rewards and no punishments. Our fears of the future have no grounds.
4. We need believe in nothing, for no one will require an account of us.
5. Greater than man there is no one; therefore, whatever is greatest (i.e. God) is before your eyes right now! Look around at yourselves!

This is a disappointing conclusion to eighteen months of hard memorizing. Three days of arguments, sometimes angry, follow.

Pipo speaks for them all. "Good sir, satisfy us on one point only and you may continue to be our guru and we will follow you. Show us some proof of your powers. You have taught us no one is greater than man, and we acknowledge that among us you are greater than we are. Show us some proof of your life-giving power. We do not ask you to make us an elephant or a buffalo or a camel, just make us something small. Make us a worm."

Mastan looks nonplussed.

Pipo seeks to make it easier. "Sir, it does not have to be a large worm. It can be a small worm, even a very small worm–but we do want to see you make a worm if you are to continue to be our guru."

Mastan Singh fails to make a worm and admits he cannot do so. Pipo maintains there is a Creator who not only made a worm but also made earth and heaven, although this particular guru does not know the way to him.

Rama equips him with a fresh suit of clothes. A weeping Mastan Singh departs from Jhandran to look for another gullible community elsewhere.

The hearts of the Megs though, have been whetted towards a search for God, and the answer is almost upon them.

The ground has been prepared for the seed.

Pipo

1859

Four months after Mastan Singh's dismissal, Jawahar Masih, a middle aged Christian from Peshawar, calls at Hajipura seeking employment. He reads only tolerably well. He has Hindu relatives in the southern part of Sialkot district that he wants to evangelize. He carries a note of recommendation from a missionary upcountry. "Jawahar has few wants and is a true lamb."

Certainly to Gordon, who talks at length with him, he seems humble, simple, unselfish and earnest. He refers Jawahar with his own recommendation to the few converts who have already formed under his guidance the India Home Missionary Society. They employ Jawahar Masih at ten rupees a month in February 1859. He starts out to visit the villages of Sialkot district before the hot season begins in late April. He comes to Jhandran.

Just outside Jhandran on the Zafarwal road is a sugar mill where many Megs are engaged. It is close to the end of the crushing season, and the laden bullock carts bringing cane are still coming in from all directions. Jawahar has no flamboyant delivery. He simply stands outside the gate and reads to the workers. He begins reading the Gospel of Mark, from the first chapter. His audience thinks he is going to read some proclamation from the government. They listen carefully as he begins.

They soon recognize, however, that this is not a government notice but about another God. They respect him and appreciate what he is saying, but they have many questions. The words are striking home. "Speak louder, ji!" Rama seats him and gives him bread and sugarcane juice. Pipo and Fakira lead him when he finishes to the dharmsala on the outskirts of the village. They insist he must stay. He has raised many questions. Tell them about this little book. Where did it come from? Is it really true? When did it happen? How do you get a copy?

Almost all the Meg community gathers at the guesthouse after work. For three days and long into the night, Jawahar teaches them. The women and children are gathering at the feet of their

Kenneth Old

menfolk. They are quickly assimilating the interest and excitement of the men.

The questions are now probing beyond the initial elementary ones of a first hearer. Jawahar recognizes the limits of his own knowledge and understanding about Jesus and his nature. He takes Fakira and several leading Megs back to Sialkot for further instruction.

There at Hajipura, they are welcomed and diligently taught by Gordon and his fellow worker Stevenson for several days. Fakira is overjoyed with what he is learning. It all has the ring of truth at last. He is given copies of the four Gospels and of Acts, Pilgrim's Progress and a bundle of tracts. He returns home delighted with his treasure. Jawahar will stay a while in Sialkot and come again later.

Eight days later, George Scott, now well established with the Sialkot Mission, goes to Jhandran. He takes other helpers and Jawahar with him. Fakira and the others come running to meet them, bowing down and giving honor to them according to custom.

One of Pipo's cousins is being married. Three hundred Megs from all over the area are gathering for three days feasting and three days listening. The interest is deep and genuine. The wedding celebrations are overshadowed by the constant teaching, the "to and fro" of questions and answers, and by discussions late into the night.

Pipo is the first to declare himself a believer, and then eighty others, the Jhandran Meg families, do so. Then others among the wedding guests join in with their affirmations. They believe! What must they now do?

After eight exhilarating days, George Scott, on horseback, has to leave for Lahore. He will go via Narowal, the most direct route. He promises to return soon. Two small boys, one of them Diyala's son, reluctant to see him go, accompany him for many miles on foot but are recovered by Diyala.

Scott returns and pitches his tent on the edge of Jhandran, near where the men-folk gather in the evenings to smoke. Diyala, resenting the move away from the traditions of their past and sensing a loss of personal power, has stirred up opposition. He has made it clear that long arranged marriages will be thrown into jeopardy.

Eighty Megs declare readiness for baptism. However, there are conditions:
- They are allowed to limit marriages to their own caste.
- Their marriage ceremonies remain unchanged.
- They should be allowed to work on Sundays.
- They be allowed to acknowledge their old religious leaders and gods equally with Jesus Christ.

Scott disagrees. No man can cross a river on two boats.

Division now develops between the Megs.

Pipo, his cousin Fakira, and a few others are willing to forsake all for Jesus.

A majority turns back.

Now it is the Muslim landowners who are putting pressure on Pipo and his companions. If their serfs become Christians they will cease to work on Sundays. They determine to drive these new Christians out of their village homes. They forbid them to draw water from the village wells or to participate in any of the village privileges.

Pipo and Fakira are beaten up–Pipo so violently that he lies ill for six months. For a while all hope of his recovery is lost, but slowly his body mends.

Diyala and the traditional Megs also take up cudgels against them. This opposition from inside their own community is hardest to bear. These are their friends and relatives. Their leaders meet in council and decide

1. Pipo and his party must prepare a feast at their own expense, and invite all the Megs of Jhandran and the neighboring villages to come share in it.

2. They must return all Christian books they have received from the missionaries at Sialkot.

3. They must cease to have anything more to do with the missionaries.

There will be a firm response from their community should they fail to comply. They may not eat, drink or smoke with their former associates. They may not draw water from the wells. ALL

Megs are forbidden to sell them food, give them water or to have any dealings with them.

After holding out for one full year, Fakira and the rest of Pipo's associates are broken. They yield to the community pressure, pay a fine, return the books and cease dealings with the missionaries.

Pipo stands alone.

He has diligently kept up his reading of the New Testament. He shows immense courage. He loves Jesus greatly. He suffers beatings; he is turned out of his village home; he drinks from the chhappard, the village sewage pond; he subsists like a dog or a jackal on whatever he can scavenge or find to eat. Bhajna, his brother, leaves him food where he can find it.

Fakira, broken from his faith in Christ, is once again hoping to reinstall himself as guru to the Jhandran Megs.

It is April 1860. Up to a dozen visits have been made by the Sialkot missionaries and workers to Jhandran to encourage the believers, but this will be their last visit for some time. Stevenson, Gordon and Elisha Swift, Scott's brother, pitch tents a mile from Jhandran.

Pipo and Bhajna visit the tents secretly at night. Pipo is deeply discouraged. Is it not possible to be a SECRET Christian?

"We taught him," writes Gordon, "it is necessary to confess Christ before the world that Christ might acknowledge us in the great day."

Pipo thinks long and hard. After the night is far spent in encouraging him by teaching, counsel and prayers, he returns to his loom and his New Testament.

Without formally professing the Christian faith by baptism, but loyally true to his affirmations, he keeps the New Testament open before him on his loom. All know he is a Christian at heart. For years he continues to read and meditate and tell the good news to all comers as he has opportunity.

In the fall of 1862 a poor, half naked man comes one day and seats himself before Gordon's house at Hajipura. He asks for a tract on pantheism. Gordon gives him a gospel. He already has that. He brings several others. He already has those. Gordon brings a refutation of Mastan Singh's doctrines. "That's what I want!"

Gordon asks how he has come to know about these things. He has been taught by Pipo. "But do you live in Pipo's village?"

"No, my village is six miles from Jhandran, towards Shakargarh."

"Are there any others in your village who think on these things?"

"Yes, there are ten of us."

In the hot season of 1866, Pipo is laid up for nine days by an attack of fever. He wastes away before the eyes of his family and friends. On that ninth day, knowing he has little time left to live, he calls together his wife, his near relatives not inclined to Christianity, and all those intimate and dear friends whose sympathies have been with him in his religious situation. He takes special care that none whom he wants present are absent.

Bhajna, his younger brother, Kanaya, Kalu, Channu, Chabbu and five others, all seekers like Pipo, are there.

They assemble around the dying man's bed. He solemnly exhorts them all to believe in and to follow Jesus. He calls Bhajna to his side and points to his own wife and four children. "My brother, these are no longer mine. I leave them with you. Where I am going, will you meet me there, brother?"

Bhajna replies "I know not how it is in my power brother to meet you after death."

"We can meet there through Jesus Christ if you believe on him," says Pipo in a whisper, raising his finger heavenward.

"If you are sure of this thing," Bhajna struggles back his tears, "then put your hand under my arm."

Pipo, aided by his brother, places his hand in the desired position, and with a struggle to speak affirms, "I confidently believe that Jesus Christ will cause us to meet again, and we shall dwell together in one place."

Those are Pipo's last words. His arm drops back. One journey is done.

Another, Bhajna's, is just beginning.

Kenneth Old

Long Walks For Bhajna

One of the young boys who goes running after George Scott when he leaves for Lahore after his first visit to Jhandran is Pipo's younger brother. Bhajna is only ten, but there is something winningly attractive in Scott that he loves. The man's dialect is different, his eyes sparkle, his enthusiasm is compelling, and he couches his teaching about Jesus in terms and stories the boy can understand. The youngster is small for his age but sturdy. With his friend, he runs happily alongside the gray pony until Diyala catches up with them twelve miles from home, beats them, and returns them to Jhandran.

Bhajna is twelve when he is married to Gulabi, who is three years younger. She is from a Meg family in Bariyan, a village towards the Kashmir foothills. After the marriage, Gulabi remains at home with her parents until Bhajna can come and fetch her when she is old enough.

When Pipo becomes virtually isolated, Bhajna is his loyal friend, companion and encourager. They sit down beside the looms under the neem tree, and while they weave, they talk. All day they talk. Pipo is Bhajna's teacher. It is not only the Gospel he is teaching. With a stick he draws in the dust the signs that are in the book. Syllable by syllable, word by word, Bhajna is learning how to read. He is quick to understand. He has many questions, and the answers are instantly locked in his mind and memory. He borrows Pipo's Gospel. With great excitement, for the first time he picks out the words that he has heard from Jawahar at the sugar mill. He labors hesitatingly through those early verses. Pipo is as excited as he is. It is not long before his hesitancy is overtaken by fluency. He practices continually. The community has more than one reader. Letters are brought to Bhajna to read when Pipo is not available. Now, too, he is becoming able even to write replies.

Bhajna's parents, Joala and Sanakhi, are not particularly troubled by the beliefs of their two sons. But like the other members of the extended family, they are torn by the isolation imposed upon Pipo. It affects them also, as if they are to blame. Pipo has a mind of his own, doesn't he? It would have been better, they feel, if Fakira had remained as their guru. Then these divisions would not have arisen. Pipo's wife Raisham also has little sympathy with her husband's self-chosen isolation. She is gregarious by nature, and the harmony of both her own family and the whole community of weavers is surely more important than which god they worship.

Bhajna now finds himself leading the group that previously had been meeting secretly with Pipo. Although the youngest of them, he can read so naturally that he is their leader. Sometimes six of them, sometimes up to ten, meet secretly in a secluded garden where he reads to them and leads them in prayer. Recognizing the value of their also being able to read, he begins to teach them by the way that he has learned, by scratching with a stick in the dust during the full moon. (There are not long twilights such as occur in more northerly latitudes during the summer, but an Indian full moon has a startling brightness.)

George Scott, tenting in Dhamtal a few miles to the south, cautiously comes up one day to Jhandran, not knowing of Pipo's death. He finds Bhajna weaving alone under the neem tree. Bhajna, delighted with his visitor but careful in company to exchange only pleasantries, accompanies Scott back to Dhamtal, along the way telling him all that has happened and is happening. Scott gives Bhajna a Gospel of Matthew and Pilgrim's Progress. These he keeps wrapped in a special cloth he weaves for them, and succeeds in keeping them as his personal treasures throughout his life.

Eighteen of the Jhandran Meg families, three quarters of the community, now move three miles north and one mile east of Zafarwal to build a new village, Naya Pind. This is to avoid the enmity of the landlords who are increasingly oppressive. Few among the families that move are Christian or have Christian interests. In the second year of the village, Bhajna and Kanaya–Rama's son–also migrate to Naya Pind.

It is the late hot season. Scott hears Bhajna has moved to Naya Pind. To visit him he crosses the flooding Deg in a dholi, a palanquin carried by two, sometimes four men. Although Scott can preach openly during the day, he dares not, because of opposition, stay in Naya Pind at night, though his friends dearly wish to afford him hospitality.

Instead Scott lodges in his tiny palanquin in an incomplete government building on the edge of Zafarwal, fighting rain and mosquitoes. Bhajna and Kanaya visit him after dark. He fetches a little diva (a lamp of burnt clay), adds oil, lights the wick with a borrowed flame and teaches the two young men until midnight.

Bhajna promises that when his wheat seed is sown, usually completed by early November, he will come to Scott in Sialkot. He is reaching the point of decision.

One night, in the garden under the bright moon, the six friends who are present–Bhajna, Kanaya, Channu, Chabhu, Ganesa and Bhajna II–resolve that no matter the consequences they will declare their Christianity. Let what will happen, happen.

Within the month, Bhajna has completed the preparation of his ground and the plowing with the two oxen. The flat board has been dragged over the ground to smooth it, and the seed broadcast by hand in the pattern of centuries.

Now, early in the morning, he sets off for Sialkot. None of his family knows where he is going. Although he is living only twenty-six miles from the town, it is his first visit there. He is not sure quite what to expect. Zafarwal is the biggest town he has ever been in. The journey takes a full day of steady walking. He is lost, arriving at the cantonment miles away on the north side where the redcoat British soldiers and the native Indian soldiers are garrisoned. Eventually he finds first the town, and then Hajipura to the southwest. He has had nothing to eat all day and had slept little the previous night.

Scott, he is told at the mission compound, is camping somewhere near Ugoke six miles west of Sialkot, towards Wazirabad. Without pausing for food or rest, he sets off on a path across the fields in search of a tent and Scott. The light is fast fading as Bhajna sees and breaks into a run towards the tent, and the man hurrying from his meal table to meet him. Scott feels like a father to the young man, and they embrace in such fashion. Bhajna has walked thirty-six miles without food other than a piece of sugar cane. He has kept his promise.

It is only after the hurriedly prepared meal that they talk about Bhajna's errand. "I have come to you as I promised. As you are, so am I–on Jesus' side."

As they talk, they agree Bhajna should try to obtain his wife before he is baptized. He leaves the following morning. Back home, he tells his loyal friends that within ten days he is going back to Sialkot to be baptized in the name of Jesus and to openly celebrate his faith, whatever the consequences. He has promised the pastor, Padri Scott.

Now comes a joyful word of encouragement. Kanaya, son of the lambardar, is twelve or thirteen years older than Bhajna. He has only had seventeen days schooling, but he has taught himself to read Urdu (the principal language of Pakistan) in the Roman script. He is a man of few words and kind hearted, even-tempered, and full of courage. He is firm and resolute once he has decided upon a course of action. He is married to Ramdei, and they have five children. He declares he will accompany Bhajna to Sialkot, come what may–and come it surely will! "I will be a Christian too, along with you." Throughout their lives, these two men remain firm friends, supporting and encouraging each other.

Channu, the same age as Bhajna, would also have come, but his wedding approaches. However, his wedding can provide the subterfuge whereby the two others can get away unnoticed to Sialkot.

Bhajna goes on to Bariyan. Gulabi is beautiful and now a woman. Her parents will not let her leave without new clothes. She cannot come. Reluctantly, Bhajna returns to Naya Pind without her.

Channu's wedding will be at Dulham, the bride's village, ten miles along the Sialkot road from Zafarwal. It is unthinkable that his two friends not be present at his wedding. The wedding party, almost two hundred strong, is strung out along the track for almost one mile, encouraged by tablas (small drums) and dholkis (large drums), flutes and pipes. Channu, suitably masked and decked in wedding garb and on a white horse with a small boy clinging behind him, is in the vanguard. They set off not long after dawn. It will be a three-day celebration.

It is mid morning on the second day. The time has come. Kanaya needs to get some wheat seed from Gadgor, and Bhajna needs wool yarn he has not been able to get in Zafarwal. They excuse themselves and keep on going through Gadgor towards

Sialkot. They step out briskly. Time is not on their side.

Disappointment meets them when they arrive at Hajipura. Padri Scott is out in camp at Sambrial, on the west side beyond Ugoke towards Wazirabad. They stay at Hajipura overnight, breaking their caste by eating a Christian meal, and thus ensuring their own untouchability.

They leave before dawn; Bhajna already knows part of the way and at Ugoke is the main Wazirabad track. Twelve miles later they are inquiring in Sambrial. He has gone to Wazirabad. Fourteen miles later they are searching Wazirabad, on the Grand Trunk road. He is not to be found. They meet no one who has seen him. Bhajna remembers Padri Scott has said his brother Elisha is in Gujranwala. That is south a further twenty miles.

Halfway there at Ghakkar it is nightfall. The night is cold and they pull their thin blanket cloaks around them. A reluctant woman makes bread for them from the flour they purchase, and they sleep in a cattle shed beside the well. By sunrise they have already been walking several hours and are on the edge of Gujranwala. They find Padri Elisha Swift's house. He is away in the district camping. Padri Scott is probably near Daska, on the road to Sialkot. Fifteen miles later they have reached Daska. Halfway there they have seen the place where the tent had been pitched last night. They are getting close. At Daska they are told he is heading back toward Hajipura, fourteen miles away. Six miles farther on, having almost completed the circle and having walked one hundred miles, they catch up with Scott.

Scott is ashamed he has not, as he had arranged, waited for Bhajna. Punjabi time is flexible by hours and by days–sometimes by weeks and months–but Bhajna has kept his previous promises. He should have known. Scott, all the while preparing them a meal, reproaches himself.

Once back at Hajipura, Kanaya and Bhajna are inducted into an inquirers' class to prepare them for baptism.

It is not many days before five men arrive from Naya Pind. There is cousin Fakira, the Christian sampler and taster and would-be guru to the Megs who had once himself been so close. There is Bhajna's father Joala, there is Diyala the co-lambardar and there are two others. Blandishments, persuasions and threats are offered. The two men decline to be persuaded.

After Diyala and his company leave unsuccessful to return to Zafarwal, Bhajna and Kanaya beg Padri Scott to baptize them. Until they are baptized, the pressures will remain on them. Once they are baptized, the irrevocable nature of the step of faith change will be recognized. The opposition then will move into a different and probably more dangerous form, but they need to move on through it if they are to come out on the other side.

On a convenient and early day in November 1866 six men, among them the two from Naya Pind, are baptized at Hajipura. Kanaya and Bhajna are the first two Megs to be baptized by the Sialkot Mission, although Pipo has been their exemplar. Their story is not over. It is just beginning. What of Ramdei and the children and of Gulabi?

Kanaya And Ramdei

1867

Kanaya, as son of the lambardar Rama, has always had status in his Meg community. He has married Ramdei, and they have five children. The marriage is a happy one, for Ramdei is a strong character who loves her husband and loves her children. They live at Naya Pind, northeast of Zafarwal. They are both slightly taller than average, of good appearance, and make a handsome couple. Kanaya is in line for lambardar, to replace his father.

Last November however, Kanaya had gone off to Hajipura, Sialkot with Bhajna and was baptized along with him and four others. When he returns, Rama publicly humbles himself before his son and begs him to return to his old faith. Diyala, the co-lambardar, does the same, and so too the other elders of the community–to no avail.

Next comes the trial of immediate family as Ramdei, weeping before him, appeals to him to return to her. The four older children–Basso, Lahnu, Gandu and Makhan–cling to their father's legs, not understanding why he is choosing to separate himself from them when they love him so much. Again Kanaya is firm and pleads for Ramdei and the children to join him in his new faith and find peace of heart.

After a mob altercation in which they are both beaten, Bhajna and Kanaya are forbidden by Hasan Khan, the most powerful local lambardar, a Muslim landowner, from ever entering Naya Pind again.

It is now no longer possible for Kanaya to live at home. He lives instead on the barren, infertile, eleven-acre plot of land that George Scott has just purchased half a mile south of Zafarwal. It is reputedly infested with witches. The seller, fearful of possible consequences from the riots in Naya Pind, is Hasan Khan himself. The area, Scottgarh, is eventually to become Kanaya's permanent home for much of his life.

At the same time he is denied, under threat of serious violence or even death, access to Ramdei or his children. There are rumors they are to be abducted to a far place. A desperate attempt is made to effect a reconciliation before this happens, with the whole family coming over from Naya Pind to be with Kanaya.

A secret meeting is arranged at night between husband and wife close to Scottgarh. Ramdei is willing for Kanaya to be a secret Christian and live with the family at Naya Pind, but further than this she cannot go. She returns in tears to her home, escorted by Bhajna, with no one the wiser that she has been away.

Kanaya decides to ask the British Deputy Commissioner in Sialkot to rule in court that he shall have access to his wife and children. At midnight he creeps back into Naya Pind, avoiding the two guards placed to intercept him. He makes his way through the random scattered charpais (country beds strung with ropes) in the open space before his home; it is early autumn and still warm at night. He sits down besides Ramdei's charpai and gently strokes her head. She is silently alert, knows his touch, and makes no sound as she arouses.

"Make no noise, husband mine," she whispers. "Goes it well with you?"

"How can it be so when I have seen neither you or the children for three months?" He tells her quietly of his intent to sue for the custody of the children in the D.C.'s (deputy commissioner's) court in Sialkot. Does she agree? She does.

"Go quietly with blessing, husband mine."

Next morning, Kanaya is walking the long miles to Sialkot. He procures stamped paper at the courthouse and engages a scribe to write his petition to the Deputy Commissioner. The D.C. is, in addition to his other duties, the Chief Magistrate of his district.

Kanaya also engages a pleader (advocate) to track his case through the long procedures of the civil courts. The pleader, accustomed to a culture of and participation in the fruits of bribes, in a hurry for his initial fee and impressed by his plaintiff's urgency, pulls strings, short-circuits processes and gets an early date for the hearing only fifteen days away.

Kanaya returns to Zafarwal. Things are moving!

Ramdei is served at Naya Pind with a court summons to appear in Sialkot in twelve days as defendant in a case brought by her husband for custody of her children. Although Ramdei takes this summons with equanimity, she is the only person in Naya Pind to do so. Everyone else, Muslim or Meg, is incensed. Men go to the courts to fight cases, not women. None of the women have ever seen the inside of a kutchery (courthouse). Shame! Shame! Shame! What is Kanaya thinking about, humiliating his wife in this way?

There are clusters, gatherings and meetings; there is weeping, beating of the breasts, excitement, fist waving and anger. Are these little children–look at them clinging to Ramdei's skirts–going to be forcibly taken away and converted from their family faith? They cannot allow this to happen! The D.C. is a Christian like Kanaya. He will surely give the children to the father! What can we do to stop this happening?

The news spreads rapidly throughout the Meg community. Seven men, mostly related to Ramdei, come down from Sukhochak in Kashmir, sixteen miles away. They will take the children away to Kashmir. Let the D.C. see if his jurisdiction extends there! Before the planned departure that evening, Kanaya, filled with righteous anger and determined to save his children, is there in Naya Pind among them. Padri Scott is accompanying him as witness. He dismisses with anger the men from in front of his house and in his courtyard. HOW DARE THEY enter his house and take away his children. OUT! AT ONCE! They leave slowly and sullenly.

Once outside they shout challenges at Kanaya: turncoat, renegade, ex-Meg, ex-Hindu, and ex-brother. They will not let him work his will upon the children, try as he might. Let him pitch his money against the resources of both Megs and Muslims and see whose goes farthest! There is more than one way to stop him, and they will find ways!

They do. They bribe his pleader, who is himself a Hindu and who sympathizes with them. Each time the hearing occurs there is an adjournment. If the defendant and plaintiff are both present, then one of the pleaders is indisposed or caught up in another case proceeding concurrently. The game of delays can extend beyond a decade. Mere tiddlywinks to legal practitioners who grow fat on retainers.

Seven times Kanaya has walked those twenty-six miles

Kenneth Old

without fruit but finally, after George Scott has handed the D.C. a personal note as he descends from his carriage at the kutchery, the case comes up before Major Mercer, the D.C.

Now the judgment, addressed to Ramdei.

"The four older children must be given up to Kanaya. The infant will remain with you until it is five years old. If possible, you yourself should go to live with your husband. You can do so and remain a Hindu if you wish."

Kanaya's steadfastness has won; or has it?

Ramdei In Kashmir

1868

After Major Mercer's judgment, the opposition party is broken in spirit. This includes Bhajna's and Kanaya's fathers and Fakira. There is also among them a Muslim lambardar with deep pockets.

They prostrate themselves before Kanaya outside the courtroom. "It is done, it is settled. The children are yours. Take them, it is your right. As for your wife, she must decide for herself. Do as you desire."

Ramdei is given no opportunity to talk to her husband but is hustled away to the pleader's chambers where accounts have to be settled. Kanaya will have to wait to talk to her until they are back in Naya Pind or at Scottgarh, wherever they decide to live if she chooses to join him. The party surrounding Ramdei has also been recognizing her lack of vehemence in her own defense, and is beginning to doubt she feels as strongly as they do about Kanaya's infamy.

Kanaya spends the night at Hajipura with George Scott and his family of believers, but he is early and joyfully on his way back home the next morning. He finds himself singing. There is a bounce to his step that has been missing. The distance does not seem by any means as long this time.

He goes directly to Naya Pind. Initially he will take the children with him to Scottgarh unless Ramdei has some other better suggestion to offer.

The village is strangely deserted. No one accosts him. Strange! He has been expecting expressions of anger and frustration and has steeled himself to deal with it. He pushes the gate to his courtyard open and stops still, horrified, in his tracks. The doors of the house swing open, untended and guarding nothing. The house is deserted! Gone is all the life out of it, and with it most of his furniture. The grain garner in the main room is emptied, the stored onions, the bedding, the dowry box–everything. All are gone.

The realization that he has been somehow circumvented and tricked is a crushing blow. His shoulders sag. He offers up a prayer in the empty courtyard before going to his neighbors to start inquiries. He has to search for people to talk to. Where is everybody?

There is a studied nonchalance. No one has seen anything; no one knows anything. Perhaps Ramdei and the children have gone to Jhandran, perhaps who-knows-where. The hands, palms upward, are spread out helplessly. How might they know where their neighbors have gone? Were not Ramdei and Rama in Sialkot yesterday? They have not seen them since they went off to Sialkot days ago. The children might have been with their relatives. They had not been in their own home yesterday; they were too small to be left alone. If it had not happened previously, then it must have happened during the night. They had not even heard anyone returning from Sialkot. What has happened at the courts there yesterday? They have had no news.

Kanaya hurries to Jhandran nursing only a very faint hope. He knows his people. It is all too obvious what has happened. The simulated total ignorance of what has happened to his wife and children weighs heavily upon him when he returns to Naya Pind. They have beaten him after all. Slowly he pulls the doors closed and then the courtyard gate. Will this ever be home to him or to his wife and children again? He trudges back slowly to Scottgarh and the few friends he still has.

Prayer is continuous there, but all inquiries prove fruitless. Day follows day and week follows week, then month follows month without news. They might as well be dead as far as anyone can tell. Within ten miles of Zafarwal, no one knows anything or, if they know, is willing to tell. There is a conspiracy of silence and ignorance. Ramdei and her children and Kanaya's own father Rama have disappeared from the face of the earth.

Five long months have passed. John Clement of Hajipura, the Indian evangelist with the Sialkot Mission living at Scottgarh, has been invited to Pindori by the two lambardars there. Kanaya and Bhajna, still without Gulabi, accompany him.

Halfway there, they meet beside the roadside a family in distress. A baby in the arms of the weeping mother is emaciated and in the last stages of amoebic dysentery. The grandmother takes turns with the baby while the father stands helplessly by, waiting until they can again proceed towards Zafarwal. They are from Jhandran. A doctor there has told them there is no hope of the child surviving. They do not know whether they will get back home before he dies. The two parties recognize each other. They are relatives. It is Ramdei's sister and her husband Kalu, Ramdei's mother and the baby grandchild Piyara. Kanaya had helped rear Kalu from childhood and had given him away in marriage to his own sister-in-law.

Kalu asks John Clement to pray for the child and to give some medicine for him. If he recovers, they may have the baby to do with as they will. He is too precious to them to die. They would rather give him to someone else; he must not die.

John not only prays for him but also tells the parents to go directly without delay to Scottgarh, where his wife will help with the child. While there is life, there is still hope. Hurry!

The men continue on to Pindori.

At Scottgarh, John's wife is plying the child with liquids. While she works to save the child she asks questions. Where are Ramdei and the children? Is not Kanaya's Gandu as dear to him as Piyara is to them? Are not their hearts breaking? Is not Kanaya's heart breaking? Kalu's wife demands secrecy. No one must know where the information has come from. They are somewhere, they do not know where, across the border in Kashmir.

Kashmir is an independent native kingdom to the north, with its Hindu Dogra maharaja and a population largely Muslim. It has its own administration, and the unlimited fiat of the British raj in India does not prevail there.

Piyara is recovering. George Scott comes from Hajipura and meets privately with Kanaya and Kalu. A grateful Kalu is reluctantly persuaded. He will go to Kashmir and see if he can locate Ramdei and the children. There will be family and caste contacts with Kashmiri Megs he can follow up. He turns to them anxiously. Tell no one! No one must know or even suspect he is trying to help. Kanaya slips Kalu two rupees. If he does find Ramdei, she may be starving and would be in need of food.

Kalu is back in the middle of the night. He has been away only four days. No one has seen him come but he has news, and it is mainly not good news. Yes, Ramdei and the children are alive but . . . they are in Jandi, a village that is the center of the fiefdom of Salar Deva Singh, the cruelest tyrant in Kashmir, a man who is almost as powerful as the Maharaja himself.

His headquarters fort is in the village about thirty miles northeast, in the foothills. Ramdei is working as a menial servant to the wives of Deva Singh and lives in a small house just in front of the gates of the fort and the kutchery. There is no hope she can ever escape! She is too well guarded. They would never make it to the border.

Kalu himself has had a narrow escape. As soon as he arrives in Jandi and begins inquiries, the noise is bruited abroad that someone from the Punjab has come inquiring for Ramdei. "Kanaya has come for his wife!" The rumor speeds around the houses and into the fort. Deva Singh has Kalu arrested and brought before him. Kalu's denials cut little ice.

Deva Singh, looking "as fierce as a tiger," gives a message. "Tell Kanaya that if ever he comes here I will either shoot him or behead him, and his blood be upon his own head! People here know I keep my word!"

Kanaya In Kashmir

1868

For three months Kanaya has been doing little except praying, working on the various tasks to be done at the Scottgarh Christian colony for new converts, and wondering what next he might do.

At prayer one evening he stands up and declares his intention. "Friends, you have been counseling me it is far too dangerous to go to Jandi to try to recover my wife and children. I am only likely to lose my life without benefit to them. I accept your counsel. I will not go to Jandi. Instead I will go to Jammu itself and petition the Maharaja to allow me to take my wife and children. What is your advice?"

Zafarwal lies in the British administered Punjab about ten miles south of the frontier with Kashmir/Jammu. Thirty miles north of Zafarwal, in the foothills of the Pir Panjal mountains is Jammu, the winter capital where the Maharaja, with the powers over life and death of a feudal king, resides in the cold season. Thirty-seven miles east along the foothills, on tracks sometimes only wide enough for a single pack animal, is Jandi, where Ramdei and her children reside.

All but George Scott counsel against such a course. Deva Singh is regularly in Jammu and has close relations with the Maharaja. He will have his own body of informers in and around the halls of power. Should he find Kanaya petitioning the Maharaja to intervene into Deva Singh's jurisdiction, what hope is there for Kanaya? If Deva Singh makes a threat, his own prestige rests on its execution. He will ensure Kanaya does not return from Kashmir alive whether he goes to Jammu or Jandi.

George Scott has shown his own courage by his earlier venture into Afghanistan. He knows only his faith has carried him through and brought him safely back out again. He sees the same qualities of faith in this quiet, lonely man he has grown to love. He turns to the others. "Let him go and hinder him not. I truly believe that God will bring him through and deliver to him first his children and then his wife. Let us commit Kanaya to the will of God and be faithful to uphold him in prayer while he is away from us."

One of the attractive facets of the Indian/Pakistani character is the manner in which loyalty between two people, friends, or master and servant will transcend the differences of race, creed, color or culture.

Marie and I saw this at Rannmal where two Muslims allied with a Christian friend to ensure that he also would be able to eat at a Muslim table. We saw it at Satiali Kalan, where during Partition the Indian Christian servants and laborers fled with their Muslim masters and employers to Pakistan to make a new life together when by remaining they might have themselves occupied the land from which their employers fled. We experienced it when Sain Ahmed, a Muslim, went to protect Marie Allison from antagonistic Christians in Pasrur. And we ourselves were supported by our Muslim employees at a time of difficulty when we were unsure whom we could trust within our own community. Mohammed Afzal provided bail for Buta when none of his Christian brothers would. We knew many, among them Muslims, whom we felt would be willing to give their lives to protect us. Bitterness does not reach as deeply as love.

We see this now at Scottgarh a century earlier as Kanaya asks whether he might have the company on his journey of Kaude Shah. Kaude Shah is a Muslim, the personal servant of George Scott, and intensely loyal. His master trusts him absolutely and so does Kanaya. This matter agreed, Kanaya asks for four books to take with him: a Gurmukhi New Testament, the New Testament, the Psalms in Roman Urdu that he has taught himself to read, and a selection of Scripture verses. These books are forbidden books in Kashmir, and possession increases the hazards of their journey.

Kanaya is a good walker. He has never owned a horse, always traveling on foot. He would begin his journeys into Hajipura, Sialkot in mid-morning and arrive in the late evening showing no signs of fatigue. Those who traveled with him said he sometimes took a nap on the road without ever halting! This time Kanaya is on an urgent errand and Kaude Shah, a younger man and no mean walker, finds himself hurrying to keep up.

By sunset they are in Jammu. They find a lodging in the

maharaja's elephant stables among the mahouts, the elephant keepers. The chief mahout, Murad Baksh, happens to be a relative of Kaude Shah. There are nine elephants and twelve mahouts, all, like Kaude Shah's cousin, are Muslim.

They invite Kanaya that evening to eat with them but he explains he is an Isai, a follower of Isa (Jesus), and they would probably prefer he ate alone. They give him lentils and fresh bread from their own meal.

Before venturing to the kutchery the next morning the two travelers, Christian and Muslim, have prayer together. Murad Baksh then persuades this poor, highly uneasy Punjabi peasant to take an unusual ride around the city. He is seated in the howdah of the splendid elephant of Deva Singh that he keeps for his own use when in Jammu. After touring the streets at a solemn and steady pace, escorted by three lesser elephants, Kanaya, high and lifted up and apparently of great estate, is duly deposited at the kutchery to proceed with his plea.

The courts of this native kingdom are simpler by far than the courts of the British raj Kanaya has encountered in Sialkot, only a day's walk away. There are two judges–one a Muslim, one a Hindu–who sit on an elevated platform six feet higher than the courtroom floor. Their clerks and assistants sit cross legged about them on the floor of the platform. The crowd of litigants and witnesses, pleaders and bystanders, mills around before and below them.

The Muslim Chief Judge for civil cases is a descendant of Mohammed, Saiyad Ghulam Nabi Shah, and the Hindu Chief Judge, Pandit Simbu Partab, is a learned Brahmin. Each despises the Christian faith and approves the proscription of Christian literature throughout the state. They are both present this morning.

If any man has a case, he just pushes through the throng of people, waits until he catches the judge's eye and assent, and states his case. Murad Baksh leaves the elephants with his assistant mahouts and himself conducts Kanaya, nervous and wondering, through to the main hall of the kutchery where the judges are sitting.

Murad pushes his way forward unceremoniously. He has been here many times and knows his way around. After a while, waiting until his present case closes, the Pandit, a plump middle-aged man who is educated up to his eyebrows in native law, nods to Murad. He knows him well and invites him to make his presentation.

"Your Honor, this man has a case."

Murad steps aside and motions to Kanaya.

THE HINDU JUDGE IN JAMMU

1868

Kanaya steps nervously forward. His loosely wrapped turban indicates he is from elsewhere than Jammu city. The Pandit inquires his name and where he is from, and Kanaya explains he is from Zafarwal in Sialkot District in the Punjab.

"Then what is the case you have in this court?" inquires the Pandit, kindly enough.

"My children were secretly carried off to the Maharaja's dominions after the court in Sialkot had awarded their custody to me. Their relatives took them away. They and my wife are detained at Salar Deva Singh's fort at Jandi and are not free to accompany me back home."

The Pandit's demeanor, one of scarcely controlled annoyance, even anger, suggests that this case is not new to him but that he has heard of it previously.

"What were the reasons that you had to sue for your children's custody in the Sialkot court?"

The muted conversations in the other parts of the judgment hall all seem to drop to complete silence. Faces are turned to this interesting new case developing before them.

Kanaya sees long arguments are going to be unnecessary. He comes at once to the point.

"I became a Christian, your Honor."

Kanaya is a Hindu, low caste for sure enough, admitting to another Hindu that he has rejected the family faith of many centuries. Furthermore, that other Hindu is sitting in judgment upon his plaint. The Pandit rises to his feet. This isn't a legal matter; it is a religious matter!

"WHY have you become a Christian? Who has made you a Christian? What foolishness! Do you not know this court has power and authority to flog you and tie you up and have you thrown out of the city onto the rubbish heap! I have only to order this for it to be done!"

The Saiyad, sitting at his own table beside the Pandit,

Kenneth Old

pauses in his own deliberations, looks across at them and murmurs his concurrence.

The Pandit, having vented his anger, concludes with a conciliatory remark to the disappointed plaintiff as, the case dealt with, he turns to attend to other business.

"Kanaya, you just give the whole matter up, go back home and don't mention it again."

Kanaya does not move. Neither does Kaude Shah, standing just behind him. The Pandit, looking up from papers before him, inquires further. The case somehow is intriguing him.

"To what tribe or caste did you belong? Who was it converted you? Tell me now!"

"I am from the Megs, sir, the weaver caste, and I was taught and baptized by Padri Scott."

The Pandit, hearing this, is searching his memory as though there is something half forgotten there that is pertinent to this case before him.

"Padri Scott? Padri Scott? Is he an Englishman?" Kanaya shakes his head.

"Of what caste was he then? How many brothers did he have?"

"He comes from the Gujar (shepherd) caste, sir, and I only know the names of three of his family: Padri Scott, Padri Swift and Lala Harbhajan."

The Pandit now, almost more soliloquizing than communicating with Kanaya, is talking wonderingly.

"Swift, Scott, Harbhajan, Daniel. I know them all. When they came into the mission orphanage at Ludhiana they were all crying. Later they all became Christians. In my own presence they all became Christians. I was working there as a teacher at the mission school." The Pandit dismisses his memories but resumes his questioning.

"Kanaya, you have become a Christian. Tell me what you have gained by leaving your old religion, which has served its people well since time began, for this new faith of yours?"

Kanaya looks up. Both judges have stopped their other work. So have all those who sit on the platform. Both judges are stern and look angry. Behind him the judgment hall, almost full with people who have crowded in, is completely silent. All are waiting for his answer.

"Sir, you are important and powerful, and I am weak and only a laboring man. You dispense justice and you have the power to order me to be flogged and perhaps killed. What I have to say has to do with what happens when we die, and you may not like what I have to say. It is better, sir, that I remain silent."

The Saiyad breaks in. "Far better you had become a Muslim if you were going to change your faith, man. Instead you have become a kafir (an infidel). Do you not know we have a commandment in the Q'ran Sh'rif to kill all kafirs?"

Again the Pandit: "What have you gained by your change of faith? Look what it has cost you. You have deserted your own religion. You have done a very wicked thing!"

Kanaya pauses for a while before he responds. "Sirs, I am helpless in your presence. If you promise not to be angry with me I will answer you. I will try not to make you angry yet if I do so, or if you feel anger rising within you, please raise your hand or tell me to stop. I will halt at once."

A wave of sympathy is slowly sweeping through the kutchery. The man is SO helpless. The court police are on hand to arrest him. His very life is in the hands of the judge he addresses. He has been asked a question. Then he should be allowed to answer and be given a fair hearing. Murmurs arise. "Thik hai, ji–that's fair enough, sir. Let him answer."

The Pandit instructs Kanaya to proceed.

Kanaya Makes His Defense

1868

Kanaya has the permission of the court to speak. He also senses that perhaps Ramdei's release is currently secondary to his being faithful to present what he believes and his reasons for believing it.

He is aware of his aloneness; he knows not where the nearest other Christian might be, nor whether there is any other at all in the kingdom of Kashmir. He is however not afraid. He is aware also of the crowd around and behind him that he cannot see. They too want to hear what he might have to say. Although his words are addressed to the Pandit, he speaks as loudly as he dares without being rebuked for shouting or preaching.

"From my childhood I have been searching for salvation and the meaning of life. My father was the lambardar of our village, and many Hindu visitors and teachers passed through and were our guests. As I helped entertain them, I listened to them and asked them questions. None were able to satisfy me.

"I went to our village maulvis (Muslim priests) and beyond them to teachers of the Muslim faith, but again they were unable to satisfy me with the answers they gave.

"None I asked, and I asked many, was able to reveal the way of salvation–but now I have found it. I have it right here with me."

Both judges together–"Then show it to us!"

"If you will please not get angry with me there are two matters. One is inside here"–he touches his heart—"and that you can hear about as I speak. The other is in this book. May I read from it to you?"

"Read on."

Under his arm is his cloth-wrapped bundle he has brought from Scottgarh. He unwraps the books. He opens the book, which is written in Gurmukhi script and the Punjabi language, finds with difficulty the right place, and passes it to the Pandit. For himself he opens his familiar Roman Urdu Testament.

Conscious he is giving to the curious listeners about him the Good News for the very first time, he begins to read, slowly and loudly, from the first chapter of Mark, just as he himself had first heard from Jawahar Masih.

The beginning of the gospel of Jesus Christ, the Son of God;

The Saiyad draws in an angry breath and his eyes spark resentment and menace.

Kanaya continues:

As it is written in the prophets,
Behold, I send my messenger before thy face,
which shall prepare thy way before thee.
The voice of one crying in the wilderness,
Prepare ye the way of the Lord;
make his paths straight.
John did baptize in the wilderness,
and preach the baptism of repentance
for the remission of sins.
And there went out unto him all the land of Judea,
and they of Jerusalem,
and were all baptized of him in the river of Jordan,
confessing their sins.
And John was clothed with camel's hair,
and with a girdle of a skin about his loins;
and he did eat locusts and wild honey;
And proclaimed, saying,
There cometh one mightier than I after me,
the latchet of whose shoes
I am not worthy to stoop down and unloose.
I indeed have baptized you with water;
but he shall baptize you with the Holy Ghost.

The Saiyad seems ready to explode; the Pandit can see this is not leading where he wishes to go. He raises his hand.

"Enough reading, Kanaya. Tell us now what is in your

heart."

Kanaya again asks his judges to please not be angry at what he is about to say. He will cease if what he says angers them.

"The One whom John the Baptist has said would come after him is Isa. That is why those who believe in him are called Isais. Isa came and was met and acknowledged by John the Baptist. It was Isa who said, 'I am the door. No man can come to the Father but by me.'"

"Isa further said, 'All who climb up some other way, idolaters and suchlike, are thieves and robbers and will not find God and will be unable to enter into the kingdom of heaven.'"

"Hindus," Kanaya is looking directly at the Pandit, "believe that a sinless incarnation will one day come. Isa is that expected incarnation. He is the Savior, he alone, and there is no other."

The Saiyad breaks in. "What has Isa done that you believe in him?"

"Sir, he made lepers clean and whole and dead men live. He told everyone who would listen, 'I do these things, I am the door, except through me no one can come to God.'"

"Do you honestly believe, Kanaya, that Isa really is the only one in all the world and through the whole of history who can save us, and that all who are without him are doomed to hell?"

"Sir, I do not wish to make you angry, but it is truly so! We are all sinners. Only Jesus can save sinners. There is no other."

The Pandit has had enough. He calls a court guard. "Escort these two men outside the city and see them on their way. Everyone who hears this man will be misled. If he has his way he will pervert the whole city."

He warns Kanaya. "If you persist in teaching these things and anyone assaults you, it is you we shall punish for disturbing the peace. Be on your way."

Kanaya stands his ground.

"Sirs, I have come to you about a matter of justice. My children have been taken from me against the ruling of the courts where I live. May I be permitted to ask, what answer are you giving me?"

The answer is contributed by both the judges before whom he stands.

"Most certainly, Kanaya, you may rest in the certain assurance that you will *never, never, NEVER* by any possible means whatever, recover your children. Go, your case is dismissed!"

Kanaya: If at First You Don't Succeed ...

1868

Back at Scottgarh, Kanaya is disconsolate, worse off than before he has made his journey to Jammu. Then at least there has been a faint glimmer of hope. Now there is none at all. No matter what he might be doing, his mind is filled with the hopelessness of his situation and the love, it seems to increase day by day, that he has for Ramdei and for Basso, Lahnu, Gandu, Makhan and Rakho. He misses them so much. Does Rakho even remember him?

Somehow there must be an answer somewhere. God is faithful and God hears and answers prayer, and he has been praying, and many others are praying, night and day. The Christians in Sialkot are very aware of Kanaya's dilemma and the whole Mission district is in prayer.

Letters have gone off to the United States from Gordon since Ramdei first disappeared and people there, without any perception of the current situation or the context of events, are praying also.

Matters over the border are not encouraging. The Maharaja of Kashmir has issued an edict declaring that should any Christians entering his dominion open their books and begin preaching and be assaulted and put to death he will ignore the event and take no action. Warning enough.

A suggestion for Kanaya comes from Sialkot.

Sometimes matters pertaining to the neighboring native kingdom of Kashmir/Jammu will arise in the courts of the D.C. Sialkot. The Maharaja retains the services of an eminent advocate there to represent his interests when needed. A Christian servant of the Deputy Commissioner, who knows well how things work, informs Kanaya's friends that Advocate Q'tub Din is a good friend of Saiyad Ghulam Nabi.

Perhaps, if the advocate were to write a letter ... If Kanaya comes to Sialkot he will arrange a meeting with the advocate.

Armed with a letter from Q'tub Din in warm personal terms asking that the bearer, known to the writer, be given access to his children and that they be restored to him, Kanaya, accompanied again by Kaude Shah, sets off once more for Jammu. Behind him is a bulwark of intercessory prayer.

This time they stay with a Muslim bow-and-arrow maker that Kaude Shah has befriended. They wish to be as inconspicuous as possible. No more parades on elephants.

They are in court early. The Saiyad is present but not the Pandit. The kutchery is not yet full. The interesting cases will come later in the day. The Saiyad recognizes Kanaya. He is not angry. "What, you have come back!"

Kanaya passes over the letter. The judge reads it slowly. Q'tub Din is an old friend from his schooldays.

"Kanaya, let me give you some advice. If the Maharaja or Deva Singh should come to know that you are here again, that you have forsaken your own religion and that you want to get your children so that you can turn them into Christians also, there would be little hope for you. If you are not put to death as Deva Singh informed you, then you will certainly get not less than six months in jail, and that can be almost worse than death.

"Know this for certain: even though the heavens should be turned upside down, it is an absolute impossibility that there is any way you can get custody of your children."

Pandit Simbu Partab has entered the courtroom and taken his place while the Saiyad has been speaking. He reads the letter his fellow judge passes to him.

He has his own piece of advice. Strangely he too is not angry. There is almost empathy between the three men.

"Kanaya, you have brought a letter from our friend in Sialkot. This is not a matter of friendship but of law. If you wish to succeed you must bring a government order (hukm)."

Kanaya, visibly discouraged by the reception of the letter in which he had placed high hopes, turns to leave and with Kaude Shah begins to walk away.

"One moment, a further word for you. When you were here

before you talked of a thing of great price that you said you had found. This is a delusion, Kanaya.

"Were it really true, surely you would be happy with your wife and children. Instead, look at where you are! You have lost your family; your relatives despise you. You have even lost your father's love. The whole world treats you with contempt and curses.

"Now, if you will give up this foolish idea you have about Isa, we will return your family to you. You do not even have to return to your own village, for we will provide for your support here."

"Please, sirs, do not get angry and I can explain to you."

Behind Kanaya the judgment hall is filling rapidly. People are crowding up close to listen. He is well remembered. This promises another interesting episode to discuss on the verandahs and in the teashops. The man is persistent and seems to be willing to risk everything.

Kanaya has under his arm this time only his own New Testament.

"In this book which angered you before, it is written, 'Though a man shall gain the whole world with all its wealth and glory and lose his own soul what shall it profit him?'"

"Repeat that, Kanaya, and explain it to us."

He does so, louder than before, and explains.

"Isa, whom you wish me to deny, has said, 'If any one confesses me before men, he is worthy of me. If any one denies me before men, then I will deny him before my Father who is in heaven.'"

"All of us, even you too, ought to confess him, for he is the Son of God and the Savior of men. Even if our wealth or our children or even life itself were taken away from us, we should not throw away our own souls. Do we possess anything more precious?

"If my life is to be the price, so be it. I will neither deny Isa nor forsake him."

The Pandit has heard the Gospel and read the Bible when he was a teacher in India. The plain testimony by this barely literate, self-taught Christian reminds him and disquiets him. He interrupts.

"Say no more, Kanaya."

There is no sign of anger as he turns to the Saiyad, rather it is more wonder.

"See how they are! I know them well from my days in Ludhiana. Ask them any hard question and they will give you such a reasonable answer that it shuts your mouth. Look at us, we are both well educated and judges too, carrying much authority, yet we too are not really able to answer this man properly."

He makes his final remark to Kanaya, virtually closing the door forever on Kanaya's hopes for his children.

"A letter will do you no good. If you wish ever to see your children again, bring a government hukm."

A respectful answer from Kanaya as he turns, denied again, to head once more back to Zafarwal and Scottgarh.

"Sir, when God gives a hukm, then I shall see them. All power and authority belong to Him. My greeting of peace to you. Salaam, ji."

Kanaya: The Hukm

1868

Kanaya's fight for Ramdei and his children has moved steadily up the ladder. From his ejection from Naya Pind and the loss of his family after his baptism, the progress has been steady although slow. His appeal in the D.C.'s court in Sialkot has been successful but has brought no reward. The search for Ramdei has finally located them, guarded by the bloodthirsty Deva Singh in Jandi. Twice he has appealed to the Maharaja's court in Jammu. Twice he has failed.

There is yet one step more he can take.

He does not understand the intricacies of the delicate balance between the rights of the Maharaja of Kashmir and the British raj that controls and governs the more troubled areas of mainland India.

Alongside the directly administered areas of the raj are the kingdoms and fiefdoms of the rajahs, ranis, nawabs and other strangely named rulers that are allowed to coexist, usually with the help of appointed 'Advisers' who try to ensure things don't get out of line.

Kanaya does know that the ultimate power in the land somehow rests with the British Queen across the sea and her representatives in India.

Those representatives filter down from the Viceroy in Delhi to his State and Provincial Governors, then to the Commissioners of the Divisions into which those provinces and states are divided. The next step down meets an exceptional body of outstanding district administrators, the Deputy Commissioners. They are some of Britain's best.

There is a Deputy Commissioner in Sialkot who has ordered that Kanaya's four oldest children be returned to his custody.

Kanaya procures an official copy of the judgment and presents himself at the D.C.'s court. He requests the Deputy Commissioner to refer the matter to higher authority since the orders of the court are being impeded. The D.C. accepts Kanaya's complaint and will inform him when there is news of action.

Three months elapse. Kanaya is called to Sialkot.

The Deputy Commissioner looks at him kindly. He has been hearing about this valiant, beleaguered man from a number of his acquaintances and he sympathizes with him.

"Kanaya, you may proceed to Jammu and get your children. Go as soon as you are able."

"But, sir, I need an order, a hukm. Is there no letter? No one will hear me if I go without a hukm."

"Do not be worried, Kanaya. You may go now without fear. An order has already gone from the government in Delhi direct to the Maharaja. That hukm says simply, "Give up Kanaya's children to their father and it will be well with you. Otherwise we shall see who is able to stand, you or we."

Kanaya is uneasy. He has learned that the powerless must speak softly if they are to survive. He is not accustomed to the directness of an ultimatum. How will the haughty Maharaja, a king within his own kingdom, respond to such a direct order for compliance? There are dangers, great dangers, not only to himself but also to Ramdei and the children.

The friends at Hajipura, George Scott, the Gordons and Martin, share his unease. Either the Maharaja will submit or, just as likely, he will have Kanaya murdered and the children will disappear forever.

Kanaya's knowledge of biology has come out of folklore, but his meaning is plain. Come what may, he is going to Jammu. "When a frog dies, the dust of its body is converted by rain into a multitude of little frogs. If I shall die in Kashmir, then many new Christians may come to life there when they see how I die."

Bhajna volunteers to accompany Kanaya. No other Christian brother is willing. George Scott cannot bear the thought of losing these two precious friends, his spiritual children, in the same calamity. Bhajna can not go. Kaude Shah steps forward. Kanaya is his brother. No matter their faiths are different. He will go again. After all, he knows the way well and he already has friends and relatives in Jammu. No question, he will accompany Kanaya and together they will see what happens.

Before they leave from Scottgarh early in the morning,

Kanaya goes during the night to Naya Pind and quietly arouses Kalu. Sitting crouched besides his charpai, Kanaya tells Kalu unreservedly everything that has happened.

"Go at once, Kalu brother, to Jandi. Let no one know where you are going. When I get to Jammu the Maharaja will probably want to question my wife whether she and the children want to go with me. If that is so, then they will have to journey from Jandi to Jammu. It will be a long and difficult journey. Many people will have told them lies about me. Tell them I love them. Prepare them for the questioning. Here is some money. Give it to Ramdei."

Kalu is not anxious to go but assents to his brother-in-law's urging. He will leave at dawn. By that time Kanaya and Kaude Shah are well along the road to Jammu.

Allah Ditta, the bow-and-arrow maker with whom they had lodged on their last visit, is nervous and highly agitated. He brings them inside and closes the door behind them.

"Look, you know I am your friend, but the whole city is in commotion because of you. The Kutchery is closed and public business has been suspended. I do not know whether there is going to be war over this matter, but the Maharaja and his Wazir (Prime Minister), his military officers and chief judges and his council of state are presently meeting in the Palace.

"Not only that, but a proclamation has been issued that if any man receives you into his house that man and all his family will be put in prison. My friends, it is no longer in my power to entertain you. Please consider me still your friend."

War Or Peace?

1868

On the east side of Jammu flows the Tawi that, later on when it reaches the plains, merges into the Chenab. The two friends, Kanaya and Kaude Shah, climb down the steep slopes to a level place near the brink of the river. An old Muslim fakir (holy man), a mutineer from the Sepoy uprising of 1857, has a small hut under a tree. It will be safer to sleep near him than in some other place; leopards and jackals abound in the hills around the city. He is happy to have company but regrets his hut is only big enough for himself and his dog. No matter, they will sleep in the open under the tree.

Kaude Shah and Kanaya have devotions together. Kaude Shah is learning to read Roman Urdu under Kanaya's tutelage and finds no difficulty in mutual prayers. George Scott has accustomed him to sharing devotions together with Christians. The verse they take comfort from that first night is "the angel of the Lord encampeth round about those who fear Him." To guard their few possessions they take turns sleeping throughout the night.

The fakir is curious about his guests, but they defer telling him who they are for a while, promising to do so later.

Kanaya is anxious to go back into the city and pursue the business for which they have come. Kaude Shah counsels that they remain where they are for a few days to see how things develop. By late afternoon, however, they are both restless. They leave their possessions with the fakir. They are going for a walk and will be back before long.

On their way, while they are alone, they rearrange and exchange parts of their clothing and headgear to effect a partial disguise.

They choose not to visit Murad Baksh and the mahouts. A visit might endanger them.

The kutchery is still closed. The bazar is dead. Wherever the people are, they are not here. No horses, no elephants are to be seen. The parade ground (maidan) is empty of people, but there are three pieces of artillery in position close by the arsenal. Soldiers guard the guns. Coolies are still working, repairing the road from the arsenal. At the great Mahal, the State Council House, the long meeting is still in progress and there is a crowd waiting outside for news of what has been decided.

Kanaya speaks to a sentry at the arsenal gates, using Dogra rather than Punjabi.

"The Kutchery is closed today. Why is that? Is it a holiday?"

Does not his questioner know? He is surprised. Surely everyone knows! "Some grave affair is on hand between the Maharaja and the English. There is going to be war." No, he does not know the reason. The guns are being checked and will be tested before they are moved up to the fort. "When the council finishes its meeting, we shall know for sure whether there is going to be war. It is surely certain there will be war."

There is nothing to be achieved at the kutchery. After meandering around on the edge of the milling crowd in front of the Mahal without drawing attention to themselves, they return to the fakir who has befriended them.

Next morning, after bathing in the river and then having devotions together, the pair returns to the city. As they wander through the bazar, Kanaya recognizes a carpenter from Jhandran who is now working as head carpenter for the Maharaja. Their fathers had been close friends. Kanaya has himself been named after Hako's father. Before making himself known to Hako he asks why the kutchery is still closed.

"Some Hindu from Sialkot district has become a Christian. His family has come over to Kashmir. An order has come from the Queen of England that the children must be given up to their father. If they are given up to their father willingly that is the end of it, but if not, the treaty between the Maharaja and the British will have been broken and the British will send an army against Jammu. The Maharaja and his councilors have been talking for three days, and this is the fourth and last day for them to reply."

The following day in the early afternoon, emboldened by encouraging devotions and finding the kutchery at last in session again, they go straight to the judgment hall and stand before the two judges of the Supreme Court of the Maharaja of Kashmir.

Kanaya is respectful and waits for the nod, surprised enough, from the Pandit.

"The hukm you requested, sir. Has it been received?"

The Pandit, visibly disturbed by the boldness of this persistent litigant, rises to his feet. Kanaya hears noise and commotion behind him as people come running from all parts of the kutchery.

He hears the voices, echoing on down the corridors and verandahs. "He's here himself!" "The Christian is back!" "There he is. That's him, standing in front of Pandit Sah'b!" "How can he dare come?"

Kaude Shah stands directly behind Kanaya to protect him from the jostling crowd pressing in upon them.

"Order! Order in the court!"

The Pandit and the Saiyad instruct Kanaya to remain there and retire to the adjacent judges' chamber for private consultation with others who join them. All the while the noise behind Kanaya is rising.

"He's the one who has insulted our Maharaja!" "Because of him our treaty with the British has been broken!" "He has dishonored our religion!" "If there's war, he's to blame!"

"Order! Order in the court!"

The Pandit has resumed his seat and addresses Kanaya.

"Kanaya, this is a very serious matter. We have a very generous offer to make to you. We have the will and the power from the Maharaja to do for you as we offer. Listen carefully. We will restore your wife and your children to you. We will make you the lambardar of a village and secure to you by law its rents. If that is not enough we will give you two villages, even more if you wish them. You may live here safely among us, assured of our protection. You, on your side, must deny Isa and resume your old faith. What do you say?"

"Sir, if you will please not be angry with me, I will respond to you."

He waits for permission to speak.

The Pandit turns to the Saiyad and the others he has been consulting.

Kenneth Old

"We should not listen to what he has to say. He has already answered enough for us to understand his answer!"

The others wish to hear further. Will he really turn down such a dream offer, given by authority of the Maharaja himself? Surely this cannot be so.

"Have I permission to speak, sir?"

"Continue!"

"Sir, you have offered me much wealth and the return of my family if I will deny Isa. I thank you for the offer. Isa has given me salvation. If you will offer me something of more value than this I will surely accept. Is it possible for you to do this for me?"

The Pandit turns to the others beside him.

"I told you so. We must stop asking this man any more questions; otherwise, all that we worship will be dishonored. I know these people well. They will never deny Isa."

A voice comes from the crowd behind Kanaya.

"Pandit Sah'b ji, in the old days he would have been bound with ropes, flogged, disgraced and his hands burned by fire until he complied. That's what you should do to him!"

This has become an open kutchery with others joining in. The Pandit forbids Kanaya to speak further and instead addresses the crowd behind him that is close to becoming an incensed mob.

"I know these Christians well. If we should cut them in pieces inch by inch they would never deny their faith.

"The Hukm has come from the English that we must give the man his children. The Maharaja's council has agreed that we shall do so and the Maharaja has so ordered.

"Nevertheless, the case rests in my own hands and I have the power to trouble him or not trouble him, to honor him or dishonor him as is my pleasure! The matter is by no means yet finished.

"Kanaya. You are dismissed. Be here when the court opens tomorrow."

Ramdei At The Jammu Kutchery

1868

Kanaya and Kaude Shah have plenty to pray about. There has been progress, even hope, for the Maharaja has acceded to the English ultimatum. However, delay in justice becomes the denial of justice. The Pandit has virtually promised that he will move slowly along the road of delays as long as he chooses and this is likely to be a very long time. For the Pandit, this is a matter of defending the honor of the Hindu gods that Kanaya has rejected. The whole country will be with the Pandit in the game he is playing. Neither Muslim nor Hindu has sympathy with Kanaya. The pair must just pray for a change of the Pandit's heart.

Next morning Kanaya, to his great joy, is told that Ramdei has arrived in Jammu and that he must wait in the court until she is brought. He longs to see her. Surely she will speak in his favor.

While he waits, Kaude Shah, who has been a good student as Kanaya has been teaching him to read, takes Kanaya's New Testament and begins to read it aloud. People crowd around to listen. Some rebuke him, crowd him and hustle him before the Saiyad, shouting, "This man is reading the Christian Injil and all who hear it will be corrupted!"

The Saiyad consults, and then says, "We will put this man on oath. Let him tell us whether he is a Muslim or a Christian."

The Pandit intervenes. "Don't ask him, ask Kanaya. He is a Christian. He will not lie."

"Kanaya, speak up! Is this man a Christian or a Muslim?"

"Sirs, he is a Muslim. He is a good man and in search of the truth. When he becomes a Christian he will himself declare it openly."

The Saiyad dismisses the two men, commanding them be gone before he puts both of them in prison. But before they can leave Ramdei arrives. She has a soldier escort. She is carrying Rakho, the baby and, accompanied by her brother and Rama,

Kanaya's father, comes into the kutchery through a side door near the judges' chamber.

Ramdei and Kanaya exchange looks, looks of both love and longing. Rakho has changed so much since he last saw her! She doesn't recognize him. He turns to look back at his wife. Ramdei steps up close to her husband. She has been previously rehearsed what she must do. She takes hold of his arm.

"My husband, I am willing to live with you and work for you, and we can live here in Jammu if you wish. Only I beg of you not to confess Isa openly though you secretly love him in your heart."

Kanaya turns to the Pandit, who is approving the way Ramdei has presented the situation to her husband.

"Sir, it is for my children that I am presenting my claim, and not for my wife. Perhaps by her own wish she will come to me, but this she must do freely of her own will. As to my children, however, the case is different. They are not able to come of their own free will. No way remains for them but to be delivered to me by order of the court. Tell me, sir, will you give me my children?"

"NO! Never can I give such a decision as that!"

Kanaya's boldness surprises even himself and it leaves the Pandit almost breathless by its effrontery.

"Sir, yesterday your Honor publicly announced that the Hukm of the English Government had arrived and that this was also the hukm of the Maharaja. If you do not give them up to me now, then you are disobeying the orders of both your government and the English Government."

The Pandit is angry, very angry. He is being rebuked and humiliated in his own High Court by this Punjabi peasant! It is as though Kanaya has taken on the role of judge.

"Go away and come back tomorrow! I will keep you coming back every day until we see who wears out first."

By now, Kanaya himself is in defiant mood. He goes to the bow-and-arrow maker's shop, opens his New Testament at Mark 1 and begins to read and preach to the curious and large crowd that gathers. By now he is notorious in the city. Everyone knows he is the man over whom war has been threatened and that he is fighting the Supreme Court for the custody of his children. People want to hear what he has to say.

Court orders are issued with the threat of summary punishment, forbidding any citizens to shelter or assist Kanaya or Kaude Shah.

Saturday has come. The Pandit has had frivolous questions for Kanaya, wasting time before he adjourns the case to the following day. While Ramdei is herself unwilling to go with Kanaya, he will pass no order handing over the children.

"Come back tomorrow!"

Kanaya puts in no appearance at the court on Sunday. It is the Sabbath. He has his own worship with a group of curious visitors at the fakir's hut. The old fakir laughs at the court threats of summary punishment for those who help Kanaya. "What can they do to me? I have nothing. I am accustomed to pain and hunger. They may punish me, but you will find I am loyal to my friends."

On Monday the couple return to the court. The Pandit reviles them with abuse. Why were they not in court yesterday? This is contempt of court. Kanaya respectfully demurs. He is a Christian. The Sabbath is a holy day to Christians when it is not lawful to attend to their ordinary business. They are to spend the day in worship of God and His Son Isa.

The Pandit, blazing with anger, is moving to have them imprisoned for contempt of court. Kanaya objects. They have done no wrong. It is the judge himself who is doing wrong, abusing them in terms that even street scavengers would not use. They are not going to run away. Surely he can see that. Where is the need to imprison them?

The Pandit responds by placing them both under arrest and hurries to the chamber of the Maharaja himself to obtain authority to commit them to prison. He wants backing from the very top in this highly sensitive case.

The Maharajah is curious to see Kanaya himself. He orders Kanaya and Kaude Shah be brought before him.

The Pandit makes the charges against them. They are causing disturbances to the peace. They are preaching from their Bibles in the streets of Jammu itself. They are perverting the people and speaking against their gods and against their religion.

The Maharaja asks the reasons for their actions in contravention to his strict orders.

"Sir, with great respect, the Pandit Sah'b would have us cast into prison because indeed I did rebuke him. These Pandits and Brahmins are esteemed among your people as little gods, but they are continually using vile and abusive language to us and telling the people to do the same. I confess, sir, that I did say to the Pandit 'You who are great use bad language just as the people of the lowest and basest castes do, such is the fruit of your religion.' This is the sole reason he would have us cast into prison."

The Wazir, standing by the Maharaja, inquires of the Pandit whether Kanaya has spoken truthfully. He nods assent. The Wazir rebukes the Pandit and dismisses the whole group back to the Pandit's court without any orders to punish Kanaya, but for the Pandit to proceed with dealing with the case.

Ramdei is again brought into the court. The Pandit, to her surprise, orders her to deliver the children to their father for this is the demand of the English Government.

She protests. It is not only Kanaya who is stubborn. So is his wife!

"Only on Friday, sir, you told me in your room not to give up my children. Now you tell me to do so. This is not right for you, a judge, to act in this way. Only with my life will I give up my children."

The Pandit adjourns the case until tomorrow and orders a soldier to escort the two men beyond the city limits.

Sabbath At The Kutchery

1868

For three weeks Kanaya and Kaude Shah have been to-and-fro'd by the Pandit. Kanaya has been able to see outside the courtroom neither his father nor his wife. It is a battle of wills that is going on.

The cards are all in the Pandit's hands. He is on his home ground. He has the power. He is a past master in the art of the law's delays and the naked misuse of legal authority. He has the populace and the Maharaja and his government with him. He has Kanaya's family, the spoils in the case, in his custody. Time is on his side. Kanaya's pitifully small amount of money is diminishing rapidly. There is only a rupee and a few paise left. Only the fakir by the river's edge, living on the edge of starvation, dares give him hospitality, and that under threat of punishment.

As Kanaya journeys to and from the court, people gather round him. They have questions and they want to know the reasons for his actions. He explains that he is an Isai, and the questions lead on from there until he has his New Testament out and is sharing what it says and means. A soldier is sent to arrest him for preaching in the streets, but by the time he meets Kanaya he has resumed his journey to the court. A helpful court clerk tells him plainly that until he bribes the Pandit, ten rupees is all it will need, the Pandit will not move.

There can be no question of a bribe. *Hitherto hath the Lord helped us.* Kanaya's trust is, can only be, in God. Ahead somewhere, and surely nearer than before, there is an answer.

The Pandit rebukes the soldier sent to arrest Kanaya for street preaching. "Do you not know that Christians eat the flesh of cows and pigs!"

The Saiyad intervenes. This matter interests him.

"Is it true that as soon as a man becomes a Christian he is forced to eat both pig meat and cow meat?" There is a belief this is a Christian initiation ceremony.

Kanaya knows they are baiting him. "Sirs, Muslims eat

cow meat and Hindus eat pig meat, yet you both associate freely with each other. As for me, no one has seen me eating either kind of meat although we do not regard the eating of it as sin. Isa taught that it is not what goes into a man's mouth that defiles him but what comes out of his mouth, such as vile and abusive language."

Enough for the Saiyad. As his friend has affirmed, the man has an answer for everything. He reminds the Pandit that he does not do well to prolong the case. The whole city remains stirred up by it, and the sooner the man is gone the better. If the Maharaja should come to hear the case has not yet been settled, what then?

The case is adjourned until tomorrow, Saturday.

Kaude Shah heads for Sialkot. They are out of money. He will report to Hajipura and be back as soon as he can. Two, possibly three, maybe even four days. Be careful, Kanaya brother, until I return. There are no witnesses now to what may happen.

The Pandit asks where Kaude Shah is. He has gone to Sialkot to get money. They are very poor people. The Pandit smiles. It is always good to have no witnesses present if you are going to misuse your power. He tells Kanaya he is now very vulnerable. Kanaya knows this and wonders what the judge is now plotting against him.

Kanaya pleads with the Pandit. If the Pandit will not give him his children then please just put this in writing and he will go away. The Pandit's response is to tell Kanaya to wait until he has dealt with some urgent business. At the end of the court's business, Kanaya has had no food but dried peas in the early morning; the Pandit tells Kanaya to be back early next morning for the court hearing.

"I cannot be here tomorrow, sir, it is the Sabbath." The Pandit knows this well. They have traveled this journey before, only this time there will be no witnesses.

The Pandit pounces.

"You MUST be in court tomorrow. This is my hukm! If you disobey I will not only have you punished, but I will throw your case out of court."

Kanaya is as firm as the Pandit.

"Sir, I cannot come to the court tomorrow. I must obey God rather than man."

The Pandit has the last word. "Who is that God, Kanaya, who can deliver you out of my hands if you do not come to the court tomorrow as I have ordered you? Go, and be here tomorrow!"

He takes his Brahminical thread in his hand and swears before the Saiyad and his clerks, "I will surely imprison Kanaya and have him flogged if he does not come to this court tomorrow."

The soldier escorts him out beyond the city gates. He spends his last four paise on dried peas. These he will eat when he arrives back at the fakir's hut. He is near the end of his endurance and resources and missing the comforting presence of Kaude Shah.

Both Saturday night and Sunday night Kanaya spends under the shisham tree beside the Tawi River in lonely prayer to his loving Father. During the day he stays near the fakir's hut, alternately reading his New Testament and talking with the strangers who drop by just to hear him talk about Isa. He does not go into the city or inquire what might be going on there.

On Monday morning, preparing his little bundle to go with him, he does not know how he will fare at the kutchery or whether he will be able to get back to the fakir, his only present friend. His heart is heavy and full of foreboding. He pleads with the fakir. If he does not return that afternoon, then surely Kaude Shah will soon be back, and he must tell him all he knows. If by any chance Kaude Shah does not come, then somehow get word to Scottgarh near Zafarwal about what has happened, and may God bless us both this day.

Climbing the hill to the city gate, Kanaya is more slow than usual. He has had little sleep or food. He meets, also climbing the hill, an old Hindu friend from Zafarwal, a Brahmin, who inquires after his family and lends him four rupees to be repaid when he gets back home. That at least is an encouragement.

Now to the kutchery!

The Pandit's Night Visitors

1868

On Saturday, as the court closes and after Kanaya has left, the Pandit announces that his court will be closed on Monday. It is the day he himself is taking as a holiday. He is having a feast for three hundred Brahmin guests at his residence high on the hill overlooking the city and the river.

He has no intention of going anywhere near the kutchery this particular day.

Kanaya does not know this. He knows there is something unusual as soon as he comes in sight of the kutchery. The hour is early on Monday morning, but where are the crowds that throng the courts whenever they are open or about to open? What further trouble does this mean for him? Has the Pandit given instructions for him to be arrested as soon as he appears?

He enters the court premises. There are one or two watchmen at the other end of the verandah. No one else is present. The main judgment hall door is ajar. He peers in around the door. The hall is empty of people–except that, sitting at the other end on the judgment dais, alone, is his old implacable enemy, the Pandit.

The Pandit, smiling, not angry, seems to have been waiting for him to come and beckons him to come forward. Kanaya approaches fearfully but he need have no fear. The Pandit for some reason is in a good mood this morning. Kanaya has been expecting an explosion of anger. What trick is this? What is happening, what has happened?

Before he can express his regrets for disobeying the Pandit's order to be present yesterday, the judge himself is speaking. Kanaya can hardly believe his ears.

"Kanaya, can you not work out some way by which those children can be turned over to you without the mother being present? She has threatened to kill herself if we take them from her. How can we do it without her harming herself?"

Kanaya's bewilderment finds expression.

"Good sir, I do not understand. Only two days ago you were

saying you would have me flogged if I did not attend your court on Sunday, and you took an oath. But now I do not understand. If you are playing a game with me, sir, you must have to find your own way to turn the children over."

The Pandit is smiling, almost enjoying Kanaya's perplexity.

"I will explain, man, but first of all tell me one thing. What were you doing last night?"

Fear flashes into Kanaya's mind. Has there been a theft somewhere? Has the Pandit's own house been burgled? Is he going to be arrested for theft? This is just what people arrange for those who oppose them.

"Sir, I did nothing last night although I could not sleep. The living God whom I worship–He was I worshipping the whole long night through. There was nothing else left for me to do."

"Don't be afraid, Kanaya. Let me reassure you. I have no accusation against you. Let me tell you what happened last night. Come up here where you can hear better."

The Pandit is obviously gripped by a great inner excitement, and his attitude towards Kanaya is warm and friendly. There are only these two men in the whole judgment hall.

"Now let us talk quietly. I do not want anyone to overhear us. Kanaya, today I am having a great feast at my house and the court is closed. I have come down here to the Kutchery, especially and only, to see you and deal with your case.

"Last night I too could not sleep.

"When I had laid down upon my bed, suddenly, like as if in a dream, two persons stood before me and said 'Arise, my good man, and give that poor man his children.'

"I immediately rose and searched the room but there was no one anywhere to be seen.

"I paced the room, thinking about what I had seen, and then again lay down upon my bed.

"Before I had closed my eyes and while I lay half awake, Lo! there were the two strange visitors standing again in front of me as before. I was not asleep. I was half awake, half asleep. They said, both of them, 'Why do you oppress that man? Give up his children! Have you not received a hukm?'

"It is not necessary to repeat all that happened; it would

take far too long and I am in a great hurry. There is my oath, too. If the people hear that I have broken my oath, they will close my mouth.

"Just understand, Kanaya, that those visits were repeated over and over and over again all night long until morning came. I have had no sleep and must, as soon as I can, be on my way back up to my house. I am here just for this business of turning your children over to you. How can it best be done?"

Kanaya is still too bewildered by the sudden dramatic change in events to let his joy express itself in creative response to the Pandit's question. He holds his hands open, palms upward. "Sir, you know best what to do."

"Perhaps you do not know, Kanaya, your wife and the baby and her brother and your father are detained here in Jammu, in prison."

Kanaya is appalled at the news. Poor Ramdei. Poor others. How have they been managing for food? Why are they kept in prison without any opportunity given for him to see them?

The Pandit quite openly explains.

"We thought that if you had any chance at all to talk to them you might persuade your wife to go with you, and then our oath would be broken.

"Salar Deva Singh and I and all the members of the council have taken a solemn oath never to allow you to meet your family. This is why she is kept in prison secretly, here in Jammu.

"All are determined you shall have no opportunity at all to speak to her.

"Let that matter work out later as it will. We will not talk to any of them yet. Let us deal with the immediate matter in hand, the Hukm.

"I suggest you come up with me immediately to my residence. I have a sheriff there. He will give you a soldier who will go with you to Jandi. When that soldier sees you and the children over the border into British territory and returns to inform me here at Jammu, I will release Ramdei and those with her.

"I cannot stop now to give you longer explanations, Kanaya. My business at the house presses upon me. Let me just say I have decided to break my oath in this matter of your children, but if others hear of it they will certainly not break theirs. You must be on your way as soon as possible.

"I am not deceiving you. I have experienced much this past night that I cannot explain." He looks Kanaya straight in the eyes and speaks with deep sincerity. "Let me just tell you this also. I confess this to you and only to you, Kanaya. He in whom you believe and whom you worship is the True God. Let us be going!"

The Saiyad comes into the judgment hall. He is surprised to see the Pandit with Kanaya and the Pandit in a jovial mood. He hears and approves the plan the Pandit reveals to release to Kanaya the children. Yes, this is well. The whole city is in uproar over this matter and the sooner it is settled the better. Some of the things this man has been saying are being repeated as truth in the bazar and by the servants. It is good he soon be gone.

The sheriff is instructed by the Pandit to furnish Kanaya with a letter and a soldier escort. He, a Sikh, is reluctant to do so before he has publicly refuted the claims this unlettered man has been making about the value of the Sikh, Hindu and Muslim faiths. A loud and bitter argument he gives, while quietly Kanaya answers as he has done previously. Kanaya is not afraid. The Pandit is anxious to see him on his way so that his preparations for the feast can proceed uninterrupted and will see him off as soon as possible.

The letter is written, read and revised by the Pandit, sealed with the official seal, and placed in the hands of the soldier to deliver in Jandi. Kanaya is advised how much he must pay the soldier for each day of his assigned duty. The Pandit dismisses him cordially and wishes him well upon his way.

The soldier will not permit his return to the old fakir. They take the high road through the mountains eastwards to Jandi.

Kanaya In Jandi

1868

It is mid-August and the rains are heavy. The air is hot and humid. There are intermittent downpours as the deep purple-black clouds roll along the foothills westwards. Most of the streams tumbling to the plains are easily fordable, but crossing them on the Jandi road in mid-monsoon season is to struggle against torrents strong enough to knock an elephant over.

Kanaya has been without his regular food for three weeks, and for the past few days has subsisted on virtually nothing except dried peas, bread and water. He has slept little, and every step now becomes an effort to a man who a month ago would have eaten up the miles in long strides without a thought. He needs frequent rests. His head aches. His feet are swollen and painful. He is getting weaker as the miles slowly slip behind them. He is a shadow of his usual self.

None of his friends know where he is, and the soldier is impatient. It is already afternoon and they have only covered five miles.

Kanaya can go no farther. Come what may, his whole frame aches for sleep. The soldier takes four day's wages from Kanaya, leaving him with almost nothing. "I will take the left fork up the hill and visit my friends while you rest and catch up your strength. Do not delay. You go straight on; the road goes direct to Jandi. I will meet you there tomorrow evening as the sun sets. Be sure to be there. We will meet at the gate to Deva Singh's fort."

Kanaya rests only a short while. His mind is forcing his ailing body forward. The sun is up until eight P.M., and he must continue while it is yet light. His body is alternately chilling and fevering.

At Scottgarh, news is anxiously awaited day by day but does not come. Bhajna goes to Sialkot to talk with Padri Scott. He will go to Jammu and search for Kanaya. He speaks the Dogra dialect well. He will be all right. On his way to Jammu he passes, but does not meet with, Kaude Shah on his way with news to Sialkot and to obtain money for Kanaya and himself to continue.

Bhajna searches the bazars and asks questions at the kutchery and the elephant stables. People are well informed about Kanaya but he has just disappeared. He must have gone back to Zafarwal. Bhajna remembers Kanaya telling of Allah Ditta, the bow-and-arrow maker. Allah Ditta, when found, can help little. Try the old fakir down by the Tawi river. The fakir is going to keep his promise to inform Scottgarh about Kanaya's disappearance on Monday. He had gone up to the kutchery with the threat of summary punishment hanging over him and had not returned. The worst must have happened.

Back to the town for more inquiries, but no news. Kanaya has disappeared.

Bhajna returns sorrowing to Sialkot to inform Padri Scott and then returns to Zafarwal. He has walked more than a hundred miles in search of his friend and has only bad news to return home with.

Just before nightfall, Kanaya reaches a village midway between Jammu and Jandi. For many miles, every step has been an act of will overcoming weakness. He can go no farther. He inquires whether any Megs live there. Yes. Two brothers with their families live with their enlarged family on the Jandi side of the village. He makes his way to their home. The women folk make him welcome when he explains that he is an Isai' Meg. They assume that is some sub-caste of Meg. Yes, he can stay overnight. He brings honor to their humble home. They can see he is fevering. They give him food although he has but little appetite.

The two brothers are away. They are in Jammu. They had a while ago escorted a Meg woman from Zafarwal now living in Jandi to Jammu. She had stayed with them on her journey from Jandi together with her baby, her brother and her father-in-law. She had had a court summons to Jammu. The brothers had friends there who might help her and after all, they were all weavers, weren't they. They had not heard of her for some time and, concerned, had gone together to inquire about her.

They talk on. She has left behind her other children in Jandi. Their mother said they all had fever. The youngest of those seemed likely to die when she came away, but she had had no choice but to leave her. She cried much of the time.

Now it is Kanaya who cries. The family is kindly. He tells them he is that woman's husband. They are not angry he has left the Meg faith but curious and sympathetic. Those sick children left in Jandi need their father. May he find them all recovered when he arrives. They help him with provisions for his journey.

Two miles before he reaches the fort, he reaches the village of the same name. He inquires about the children. Although they are in the same street of the village where he is inquiring, no one tells him they are there. This is where Bhim Sain lives, son of Deva Singh, and no one is going to risk his wrath by informing Kanaya his children are within the servant quarters of his courtyard.

He goes on to the fort. There is no sign of the soldier escort. There will not be for another two days. He identifies himself but meets no anger from the guards. The children are back in the village he has just passed through.

Returning down the hill, who does Kanaya see to lift his heart into the skies with joy but a little boy, thin as a skeleton, running towards him and crying "Abbu! Abbu!" (Father! Father!) Kanaya too breaks into a run–his pain, his weakness, his tiredness, his fever all forgotten–and lifts the child high into the air then hugs him close, crying as though his very heart would break with joy. "Oh Lahnu, Lahnu, my son, my son, my son!"

Bhim Sain has come running. He stands at his threshold and defies Kanaya to cross it to embrace either Basso or Makhan. Both girls are seriously ill and lying helpless on the same charpai. He can see them both. Makhan, his little joy, his rose, is listless almost to the point of death.

The children brighten to know their father is at hand. Gandu receives the same embrace as Lahnu. Now Kanaya needs to wait and do what he can for the children until the missing soldier escort arrives with the orders from Jammu for the children's release. All the children are near skeletons from lack of food and severe sickness. Other servants in the household are kind to the children and doing what they can. They dare not offer Kanaya hospitality; they do not know what has happened to Ramdei since she left almost a month ago.

Kanaya is a survivor and somehow, almost completely penniless, survives now also. He finds no friendly fakir by a riverbank, but people do leave food where he can find it and make no objection to his drawing water from their well.

The Jammu soldier at last arrives and the order is presented at the fort. The order is accepted. It has the Maharaja's seal. There is no dispute. Kanaya may take his children, and good riddance to them. It is early evening. Because of the heat they will travel by night. Fortunately the moon is full. He places a bamboo upon his shoulder and suspends from either end a tiny bed-cum-chair for the two sickest children. Basso is nine and Makhan five. Lahnu and Gandu can walk although they are not strong. He bends to place the bamboo in balance on his shoulder pad and straightens himself slowly and with difficulty. He is ready to start. There are thirty miles to walk but they will go slowly. "It is not far, my children."

It is not far, for they are going home!

Bhajna And Gulabi

For many who make the choice out of a different faith to walk the way with Jesus, the hardest point on the whole journey is the loss of the immediate family and its affection and support. There were a number of men in or of Jhandran who reached that ultimate point.

Pipo, the first to come, reached that place, and passed through to the other side, but did not dare the seal of baptism that would have been his defiant witness to a local world bent on destroying him if he dared continue on. One day someone will erect a deserved memorial to this forgotten and faithful herald of the Christian faith in Jhandran.

To some, like Channu and Kalu, the journey was a slow one but steady. They did not move at the pace of Kanaya and Bhajna, but they traveled the same route and as certainly–through opposition, family alienation, violence or threat of violence. Inevitably came the crisis encounter and the decision that entailed a period of utter loneliness and dependency.

Rama - Kanaya's father and Joala and Sanakhi - Bhajna's parents eventually came through. Others like Nattu and Lalu reached that point in a tortuous journey which included a reversal of direction and turning back several times before eventually breaking through into the sunlight.

Fakira, Pipo's cousin and erstwhile guru to the Megs, reached the point of decision several times and hesitated. He never found the courage to venture that final step. On his deathbed in agony of soul, he called his family and friends close near. "I have denied Christ and am lost. Beware lest you also come to this fearful end. Believe on Jesus Christ now!"

Nattu, Fakira's brother who had so determinedly opposed the claims of the Christian faith, was haunted by Fakira's death and dying admonition. In 1881, twenty years on from Jawahar Masih's visit to Jhandran, he brought his wife and five sons with him to baptism.

Another equally affected by Fakira's death was Lalu, his nephew. He vehemently opposed Kanaya, Bhajna and Pipo and helped lead the protests and reactions against them. In midsummer 1880 he returned from Amritsar to resume living in Jhandran and was baptized. His wife, rejecting his action, left to hide in Kashmir with her infant son, but three months later returned and was herself baptized.

Kanaya, the brave and stalwart, walks steadfastly all the way into the blizzard and comes out unbroken on the other side to be eventually joined by those he loves, first Ramdei and then his father.

Bhajna, Pipo's brother, younger than Kanaya and mentally not as bright and clear of mind, is equally stalwart, but the outcome of his story is to be very different. It deserves looking at again.

Bhajna is twelve when he is married. His bride Gulabi is three years younger. He likes the suitably shy little girl he is marrying. Gulabi remains behind with her parents to reach maturity when Bhajna can come and take her.

Raisham, Pipo's wife, stays with her husband's family after his death. Bhajna, now seventeen, has responsibility for her and for the four children. Raisham stays resolutely throughout her life outside the Christian faith. By now, Bhajna and his father are building the room on to the house for Gulabi and himself that they will occupy. He will soon be going to fetch her.

As they work, Bhajna talks with his father about baptism. Joala, nicknamed Doana (Tuppence), is not happy the conversation is going this way or that it repeatedly returns to it. He remembers what happened to Pipo. Both he and Sanakhi, sympathetic at heart, are deeply anxious about the possible consequences. They are not prepared to be baptized themselves or to allow their son to be baptized.

It seems wise for Bhajna to first ascertain whether Gulabi can come back home with him before he is baptized.

Bhajna goes to Bariyan. Gulabi is beautiful. She is now a woman. Their eyes feast on each other. Gulabi's parents will not let her leave without new clothing. Yes, she is of an age, but it will be shame for them if she goes without new clothing. The tailor will take at least two full weeks. The more Bhajna urges, the more firm they are she shall not go without new clothes. She cannot come. Reluctantly, Bhajna returns to Naya Pind without her.

At Channu's wedding, which will create the opportunity for the two men to break away to Hajipur for baptism, Kanaya and Bhajna join in the banter and the laughter but their hearts are heavy. They face separation from and rejection by the people who in the entire world mean the most to them. Bhajna is wishing he could be bringing his bride, new clothes or not, to meet and be met by all the Megs at the feast.

Once baptized, Bhajna has even less hope than before of soon obtaining Gulabi. Kanaya is losing his wife and children, but Bhajna has never even possessed his wife.

Again he goes to Bariyan. Lado, Gulabi's mother, loves Bhajna as though he were her real son. She is sweet tempered and gentle. She is willing for Gulabi to go with Bhajna even after his conversion, but her husband is less easy to persuade. Lakhu is Gulabi's father, resolutely opposed to Christianity but a man to be respected. In time he might be persuaded. The real determining power in the family clan, however, is not Lakhu but Rura, the husband of Lado's elder sister.

Rura is a bear of a man, heavyset, coarse, and burly with a huge black beard. He is ambitious, officious, hot-tempered and overbearing. Rura lives just over the border from Bariyan, in Kashmir. He follows Mastan Singh's teachings. He is not going to let his sister-in-law's daughter be trapped by the marriage commitments that were made for her as a child when they were made in good faith to a Meg family of good standing, and distant relatives at that. The circumstances of Bhajna's conversion have completely negated all previous commitments.

Bhajna, following Kanaya's example and with his advice, enters suit in Sialkot in the civil court for Gulabi, his wife. Padri Scott is a constant help and adviser to them and as the hearing approaches there is much prayer in Scottgarh and Hajipura.

Rura is as determined as Bhajna. He is representing the Megs in the defense of their faith. He has taken over the response to the suit from Lakhu, who is merely a compliant passenger. If Bhajna goes unchallenged, where will it all end? Perhaps Kanaya has succeeded. Bhajna never will!

Rura has his contingency plans for Gulabi. She is already across the border and staying with her senior aunt. Not only the total Meg community, but also local Hindus and Muslims are contributing to the legal defense fund Rura has established. The network of bribes and promises is already well under way. If the worst happens and the verdict goes in favor of Bhajna, let him just try and find her. Kashmir is too large a state for him to visit every village, and they are not limited to Kashmir. Bhajna will be fighting against the whole Meg community.

The verdict is given in favor of Lakhu. Bhajna's suit is dismissed. Bhajna is brokenhearted.

Rura is elated. Now to finally resolve the situation. He knows that Gulabi loves Bhajna, and the opportunity has come for the deals and negotiations from a position of strength that is the heart's blood stimulus to the true Punjabi.

Lakhu and he meet with Bhajna and Joala. They have refused to allow Kanaya to be present. If the deal is to be successful, Bhajna must remain isolated. They meet in Bariyan. Kanaya accompanies him part way.

Bhajna has had no choice but to comply with the location. He is hoping for at least a glimpse of Gulabi and some sign, be it ever so small, of her continuing affection. Lado greets him warmly. He whispers an inquiry and sags visibly to hear from her mother that Gulabi is away visiting her aunt. She has prepared a meal for the visitors and for her own men folk. They must eat first before they talk. Now the huqqa. The bargaining begins.

Rura speaks on behalf of Lakhu and is supported by his frequent nods of assent. He promises to give his wife Gulabi up to him. Furthermore, he will give him another wife in addition to her, a pretty one. All Bhajna needs to do is to deny Christ, set aside once and for all his baptism as a mistake and become a Meg again. The alternative is that he will never see Gulabi again. Try as he might to find her, he will be a hundred years old before he has visited even a quarter of the hiding places they could find for her. Kashmir is only one of the places they can hide her. Beyond is all of India.

Bhajna, more and more hopeless, can only continue to reaffirm his faith and plead for his wife to be released to him. Joala, his father, has no encouraging advice except that he accept the offer being made to him.

Brokenhearted, Bhajna returns to Scottgarh. There is nothing more they can do, and continuing prayer brings no resolution or hope of reunion with Gulabi. He has lost her.

Rura, having become a leader of high standing in the Meg community because of the successful court outcome, continues vehemently to oppose and persecute the Christians. After George Scott's death, he persecutes them with greater vehemence and determination than ever.

With all his might and cunning, he labors to bring about Bhajna's apostasy but with little hope of success. However, he will teach him a lesson he will never forget. He allows himself no rest until he secures Gulabi's marriage to another man who already has a wife and three children.

(Six months after this triumph he became blind. A little after that he lost his only son by death, and a short time after this he himself died, having scarcely reached the prime of life. However, he had accomplished the damage he sought to wreak on Bhajna's marriage. Gulabi was now the wife of another and was to remain so. Bhajna was alone. He and Gulabi were never to be reunited.)

DITT AND SHAHABDEKE

1963 / 1873

During the spring, before Marie had taken our two unsuspecting five year olds off to Murree to enroll them in the school for missionary children, she was helping in the mornings at the Mission hospital in Sialkot. There was a shortage of missionary nurses in all the mission run hospitals. Jhelum had closed with Evva's retirement, although she would stay on another decade in a rented house to care for her twelve "adopted" children. Sargodha was struggling and would eventually close when Francis Lincoln retired. At Sialkot, there were many student nurses in the nursing school but few Pakistani full-fledged sisters who could carry the burden of teaching. Glendene's furlough was already delayed although the American wife of a Pakistani college professor was helping out.

I would take the two boys, clad in their school uniform of white shirts and white shorts, on my bicycle to the convent school in the cantonment. They were not the only non-Pakistani children in the school for Irenika, the Hessels' daughter, was also a student there. They were learning to write Urdu in Arabic and to speak and recite English with a Pakistani accent.

There was a host of activities for me related to building. The dearth of cement (and/or money) encouraged the building of walls in a mortar of mud that later, to limit the effects of weathering by the monsoon rains, were pointed in cement mortar. There was a large backlog of building work. The institutions of the Sialkot Mission–schools, colleges, hospitals–had lacked a mission builder for a decade or more. The local Islamia college, which had a tricky design problem, was also seeking help.

There was also non-institutional building such as village churches. Over the years I was involved in either building or roofing many village churches, but Shahabdeke was the first of them.

It was probably Joe Alter, whom I loved like a father, who prevailed upon me to squeeze out a little time for this particular job. Just possibly he may himself have known Ditt for Marjorie, and he had come out in 1922, before I was born. Ditt would have been about eighty then. Old Channan of Tergha told me when I was roofing his church in the late eighties he remembered Baba Ditt, who had lived over in the next village. Ditt had lived to a good old age.

I have before me, as I write, a photograph of some early and influential members of the Synod of the Punjab.

Among them is Mohammed Alim, the first Muslim convert, baptized in 1873. He is a maulvi from the Jhelum district, active also as a schoolmaster. His conversion came from obtaining and reading the New Testament as though it were completely true and could be trusted absolutely.

The Muslim religious leader, Imam ud Din Shahbaz, is there also. Indian and Pakistani Christians the world over know him as author of the first popular hymnody of the Punjabi church, the Punjabi Zaburs (Psalms).

In front of the four men on chairs, seated on the floor is Ditt. He is short in stature and sits leaning against a cloth-covered bundle of books, or maybe a harmonium. He wears a puggree (turban) more tightly wrapped than the usual loose rural puggree of nowadays, folded somewhat as the Sikh turban but not as tightly or neatly. His eyes are piercing; he is lightly bearded and darker in complexion than many of his companions. He holds what is probably a New Testament. Presumably he used it as a visual aid since he never was able to read. Undoubtedly he had committed many passages to memory.

Ditt is a Chuhra.

The tiny struggling Sialkot Mission had been observing since 1866 the remarkable experiences of Kanaya and his family. They were Megs living in Zafarwal only a few miles from Ditt's village when this story of Ditt begins a few years later in 1872. Megs are weavers, and it is amongst this group of people that the Holy Spirit is working with power. Kanaya is a towering figure.

It is through Ditt, however, rather than Kanaya that the religious face of the Punjab is to change forever.

Within the outcasts of Hinduism there are divisions and

strata. The Megs are a little lower than midway on the scale of caste. At the bottom, far below them and the line marking untouchability, are the Chuhras, possibly a name deriving from the word for leather, chamra. They dispose of the carcasses of carrion, the animals drowned in the floods and defleshed by vultures. They deal in bones and in leather and horn and animal hair. They are sweepers and scavengers. They live on the lower outer edges of the village where the sullage water runs into the chhappard, the sewage pond. In Ditt's day there are over a million of them in the Punjab.

Ditt is about thirty. He is married with several children. He anchors his padded stick under his left arm in the armpit, twists his crippled leg around the stick, seizes hold of the side hand-grip, and walks with ungainly but rapid steps over to Nattu's village a couple of miles to the north. To the northeast, Mirali village is three miles distant. Punjabis are great walkers. Distant horizons are no deterrent to a visit. The land is flat. After the first winter rain, the dust has settled, the ruts that have not filled in with earth are easily avoided and, as the turn of the year approaches, the winter wheat a few inches high invites the heart to sing.

Ditt is going to check on business, but also he has been hearing things about Nattu that he wants to investigate. Nattu is the son of the lambardar, the village headman, and a cultivator from the Jat caste. He has lands. The two men have known each other since childhood. Ditt has bought from him and sold to him before and there is mutual respect and friendship.

"What's all this about, Nattu? What is it that you have done now? It's one thing to listen to these preachers who pass through, but what's this I hear you've gone and burned your boats? Tell me again about this new god you have found. What does your father say? What's going to happen now? What about your wife and the children?"

Nattu is not loath to tell his story and his answers quickly unfold. Ditt and he have talked before about some of this. Ditt has known from Nattu about the visit of an Indian follower of Yisu (Jesus) to the village. He had stayed for some days before moving on towards Mirali and then Narowal. There was a ring of truth to what he was saying. Nattu had believed what he said.

A prophet, Yisu, had lived a long while ago. He was more than a prophet. He had been killed but he had not died! He is the Son of God. He forgives sins, yes, all the sins that Nattu ever committed. Ditt is curious about this. "Even . . . ?" He mentions a particularly heinous offense that only the two know about. "Yes, even that, and more!"

Since he had last seen Ditt, he had gone in to Zafarwal where a white man new to the district, a missionary, was living for a while in that house just outside the town that they had both observed being built. The man had been friendly; he spoke Punjabi well enough to understand, although not with great fluency.

The white man treated him with respect and told him many, many new things.

Now Nattu himself has become a follower of Yisu!

"What does this mean? What about Krishna and Vishnu and Kali and Humayun and Ganesh and . . . ?" Nattu is shaking his head from side to side. Ditt's eyes grow large with the effrontery of the preacher's requirements and at his friend's own daring.

Nattu continues. "To follow Yisu it is necessary to be baptized." Nattu explains what this is. Three weeks ago Nattu was baptized, in Zafarwal, by the white man. Nattu can read. He shows Ditt the Injil the white man has given him. Nattu is reading it through bit-by-bit, daily. He opens it and reads, slowly and haltingly, from one of the Gospels. Ditt likes what he hears, but even more he likes what has happened to Nattu. This is a different Nattu–gentler, less sure of some things, more sure of others.

Nattu offers to teach Ditt about Yisu. Ditt agrees.

Through the winter and on into the spring, Nattu teaches Ditt. Many of Ditt's questions Nattu cannot answer, for he knows so little himself. But as he reads steadily through the Injil some answers become clear. Ditt is asking fewer questions as time passes; he is more interested in just hearing Nattu read. It is all making sense to him. Occasionally Nattu visits Zafarwal, once even Sialkot. While there, he finds out from the followers more about the Way.

The wheat is harvested; it is a good crop, and Ditt too is now ready for harvest. The hot season is here. The railway line has not yet crossed the Degh nullah so there is no easy way across the raging torrent once the rains begin. The nearest missionary is no longer close by in Zafarwal but in Sialkot, thirty miles away. The clouds are rolling westwards along the Kashmir hills. It is time to move.

Nattu and Ditt, traveling steadily at Ditt's best pace, ford the Degh and head for Chawinda and the next day for Hajipura, the South compound of the Sialkot Mission in Sialkot.

Sam Martin is a man more full of questions than they expect. The Sialkot Mission missionaries have reluctantly become colonists. It had been taken for granted that the new Christians, slowly emerging and being baptized (about one hundred and twenty in all after eighteen years work), will be unable to go back to their village homes because of persecution and threat to their lives. For about three years though, it has been accepted by the missionaries that in some circumstances it is possible and desirable that converts return to and live in their own villages after conversion. All attempts, however, to persuade anyone to do this have failed.

Yet when they are in fear of their lives, they have to be helped, and all too often they have families of dependents. Inevitably it means colonies around the several mission residences, and also the problems of under-employed and sometimes quarrelsome followers in close proximity and demanding attention. Nurture of the small community in their own backyard is so demanding it is wiping out evangelistic initiatives. There is so little time, there are so few workers, and funds are so limited.

What then are the motives of this cripple from the Chuhra tribe near Zafarwal, to join the club in the backfield?

Sam eventually recognizes the sincerity and humility of the little man. He is simply asking to be baptized. Should he baptize him? That is another matter. Ditt's only teacher has been Nattu. Nattu himself has only recently been baptized by Jim Barr. Will it not be wiser to keep both men with him for a while, instruct them both and use the opportunity to confirm the smaller man's sincerity?

Ditt is against this. He sees no need for delay, not even for a week's intensive teaching. Does the sah'b (white man) think he does not understand? Ask more questions then! He wants to get back over the Degh before it becomes uncrossable, and the first monsoon rains could be any day. Nattu too is urgent. They have not come to stay. They have merely come that Ditt can tell that he too believes in Yisu and that he is ready to be baptized.

Ditt responds quickly and clearly to Sam's questions. He affirms his new faith. He has few questions. Undoubtedly he understands that he is resting himself completely in the saving grace of the Lord Yisu. Nattu vouches for his integrity.

Sam decides eventually, with no clear certainty, to baptize Ditt–not out of conviction, but because he finds no clear Biblical reason not to do so.

It is June, 1873.

Ditt The Christian

Ditt is feeling good as Nattu and he retrace their steps. They talk excitedly. At their stops for rest, they take opportunity to pray in Yisu's name as they have learned. The Degh River is higher but no serious impediment yet. The sah'b at Hajipura has not wanted them to go, has advised against it, but there is after all no reason they should not. Nattu has already been a follower of Yisu for half a year. Nothing has happened to him!

Ditt has other more personal thoughts also. He carries no burden now of his sins, for is he not forgiven? What though about the whole family? Will they accept the good news he brings? Not only his wife Gulshan and the children, but also the sixty others who help make up the Ditt clan. What about all his friends and acquaintances? The Muslims won't mind a bit; probably the Sikhs won't either. But the Hindus, from high to low and most especially among his own tribe–that will be different. It won't be easy! He will tell them what he has done, but he is guessing, with a queasy feeling in the pit of his stomach, how they will react. They will not like it, he knows that. He is the very first among them to give up the old gods. He will have to persuade them. Yisu, the God who lives, will help him.

Ditt has five brothers, all in and around the Mirali area. They are furious that he has done this, rejected the tried and tested gods of their family and become a follower of Yisu without even consulting them. Who is Yisu, after all?

There is a prompt family gathering at Shahabdeke. Almost all the men and most of the womenfolk are there. It is early evening, not yet dark. The scene is filled with drama. Rope beds have been pulled out to the fringes for some to sit. In the great circle, on reed matting, the women and children and the younger men sit. It is trial by his peers.

They listen first to Ditt. He sits on a bed between the well and the banyan tree, his crutch beside him. As is the custom, they interrupt him and any others who might be speaking at will and without apology. Half a dozen sub-conversations are going on simultaneously with much gesticulating and gathering volume. The mood is one of anger. As it builds they are rising to their feet, shaking their fists, acknowledging the murmurs and shouts of agreement and disagreement. He has dishonored their parents, grandparents and ancestors. He has dishonored them. Have not their gods served them well? Why this change now? What madness is upon him? None speak in his favor.

He has hoped by this action to become one of the 'sah'b logue' (white people). Well, he is NOT and never will be. Neither will they, his blood family, accept him back even if he wants to come! He is now without any faith at all for THEY reject HIM. He is not welcome to their hospitality in the future and they will not accept his. May his other leg also become broken. Gulshan had best return to her parents with the children. They will not trade with him. If he needs any help, let him ask the sah'b logue. He will soon see what they will do for him. He must pray to his Yisu he will not become sick, because they will not help him. He must find someone else's well to draw water from. He must not pollute theirs. He deserves that his buffalo become sick and cease giving milk. His buffalo shall not eat from THEIR trough.

Ditt hears them through. It has been even worse than he expected. He looks over at Gulshan, who is sitting with her sister among the womenfolk. She looks anguished and broken. Surely though she still loves him and will stay with him. Now he is not sure even of this! Yet can he face the future without her? Rani, their daughter, sits just in front of her. It is hard to read her face. How can she understand what is happening?

"Very well, brothers and sisters, if it pleases you, you may oppose me and abuse me and cut me off from your fellowship. That is your own will. You know you are all very dear to me. I treat you and will continue to treat you with respect and love. If you want help I will give it, but Yisu is the truth. I believe that. I want you to believe it. Nothing would make me happier than that all of you should have the peace in your hearts that Yisu has given me. I cannot, and will not, go back on what I have done, for I cannot deny the truth. If I must stand alone, I will stand alone."

In August of that same year, just a couple of months later, during a lull in the monsoon rains, Gulshan and Rani and two of

Ditt's near neighbors accompany Ditt to Sialkot. He has instructed them to the best of his ability. Nattu has invited them across to his village to visit and talk. He has read to them out of the Injil. They too have memorized a few verses. Rani particularly, with her young agile mind, has memorized everything her father remembers. None of them can read. It is still mid-monsoon and there is some flooding nearer Sialkot. The Degh is full and the crossing now difficult. Ditt introduces them to Martin Sah'b. He has brought them to be baptized. They can't stay long.

This time Sam is not arguing or trying to persuade them to stay. He questions them about their knowledge of Christ, their faith in Him as their Savior and their intent to be faithful and obedient to Him and His commands. He baptizes them in the storage tank near the well and makes sure they have food with them for the journey home.

Six months later, in February, Ditt brings four men from his neighborhood. One of them is Kaka from Mirali. Kaka is Ditt's first male relative to make the journey. Again, Sam baptizes them and sees them off on their return with Ditt to Mirali. Kaka also now becomes active sharing the news of Yisu.

Kaka leads two young men from different parts of the family to Christ. They are part of the next baptism group to Hajipura.

Steadily throughout the following decade, more and more members of the family are coming to stand beside Ditt and equally take up arms in the struggle of sharing Christ with others. It is spreading now from household to household, to family clan after family clan, from village to village. Soon the movement embraces scores of villages and hundreds of families.

Simultaneously and seemingly unconnected, Chuhras, after the first one or two have taken the step, are accepting Christ in Gujranwala city and district and in Gurdaspur district across the Ravi. None of these similar points of growth, however, match that of the Mirali area. Ten years after Ditt has first gone to Sialkot, the fathers of the first two disciples of Kaka, the most violent of that initial family opposition and about the last to yield, are themselves baptized and are embraced by the little cripple standing nearby.

Kenneth Old

The Annual Meeting of the Sialkot Mission early in '84 in Jhelum reports that communicant membership of the Synod of the Punjab has almost doubled within the year to more than eleven hundred! Growth is continuing ever more rapidly.

The subsequent annual meeting in Gurdaspur reports an accession of more than five hundred during the year. There is little natural explanation. A leaven-like event is happening. There is a widespread spirit of earnest inquiry. A strange excitement is pervading the mass, widening, deepening and surging independently of the agency of the Sialkot Mission!

About this time Andrew Gordon writes of Ditt in these terms: "When Ditt now visits his people, their love to him and their joy at meeting him are as intense and unfeigned as were once their hatred and opposition.

"In scores of villages throughout the Mirali region, when differences arise between the Christian brethren, when advice is required about business, when marriages are contemplated and especially in matters of religion, the new Christians trustingly resort to Ditt as their wise and able counselor.

"Whenever he detected worldly motives in persons professing religious inquiry, he refused to bring such inquirers to the missionaries. He never asked for any financial support. Many long journeys were performed by him on foot. At the end of seven years after his conversion, it was observed he scarcely had any time left for his own business and consequently nothing to live on. Even then he asked for no help. However, six or seven rupees a month, enough to support him in the humble way these people live, were given him as his right, enabling him to devote his full time to this grand work."

What happened at Mirali and Shahabdeke was not only an immense stimulus to the work of the Sialkot Mission, but it revolutionized its methods and goals. Henceforth, it would minister to the poor and allow the educated and wealthy to come at their own speed later. They would follow and not lead. In the future, the focus would not be urban but rural. Instead of manning bases in the towns the missionaries would go into the rural districts and sow for the harvest there.

In 1873, the year of Ditt's conversion, the Sialkot Mission

had two ordained missionaries (and wives) and one single woman missionary on the field. Ten years later it has seven ordained men (and wives) and seven women.

Things have begun to move rapidly.

MOHAMMED ALIM

1967 / 1873

Our experiences with Bilquis Sheikh, whose story is told elsewhere (*I Dared to Call Him Father),* had given us much to think about.

Jim Cummings, one of the Sialkot Mission's great missionaries, was himself a Mission Kid. He once told me that in all his life in India and Pakistan, over sixty years, he had never known a Muslim come to Christ except as a result of supernatural experiences–dreams, visions, voices, healings and the like. If that were so, then Christians could hardly be accused of proselytizing converts from Islam when the clear initiator was the Holy Spirit rather than a human agency.

My own feeling is that although this perhaps was true for Jim, in the past three or even four decades a change, not of initiator but of method, has occurred. The principal agency by which it appears Muslims are now led to encounter and deal with the claims of Christ is simply by reading and studying the New Testament. This is surely affected by increasing national literacy.

Marie and I once had a cordial meal with a neighbor in Murree who was the Pir Sah'b, the Islamic spiritual guide of the ruling President of Pakistan. We discussed freely our religious differences.

He commented, "The Muslim believes in the New Testament. The Q'ran Sharif so affirms it as Scripture."

"Then how does Islam account for the differences Christians perceive in the teachings about Christ and Islam's own beliefs about Christ?"

"There are two New Testaments. There is the received New Testament that the Christians use which, as you yourself know, has gone through much translation and editing. Inevitably it will contain errors. You will also be aware that our Q'ran is without error. It was received in the Arabic language. It remains in the Arabic language. It is more than anyone's life is worth to alter even the position of a comma. These are the words of Allah. They are pure truth. In like manner there is a pure version of the New Testament and, like the Q'ran, the Original is in heaven."

"Then is there such a pure copy of the New Testament available for men and women of our own time to use?"

"Yes, there is even a copy available in Pakistan, but I am not willing to tell you where such a copy is to be found."

I went back again to Andrew Gordon's history of the early years of the Sialkot Mission and reread the story of the conversion of Mohammed Alim in 1873.

Mohammed Alim lived in Aurangabad, several miles to the south of Jhelum. It is an old town. Although it is on the Grand Trunk Road, modern changes have passed it by and it is very much as it had been centuries before. It is a walled town and has a north south street running through its center with a large gate in each wall. On the west side of the town is a wicket gate allowing only one person at a time. Outside this gate, a short distance away are some shops and a caravansarai known as Sarai Alamgir.

Mohammed Alim was a maulvi. From his three hundred families he received an income of twenty-five rupees a month for his religious services. He was also the local schoolmaster, and this enhanced his income.

In 1867, when he was 32 years old, he began to feel unworthy before God, whom he would one day need to face and account for his life.

He needed a true knowledge of God and holiness in his heart. Where would he find it? He began to seek counsel from various holy men (fakirs, sadhus, mendicants, ascetics).

Two successive fakirs of good reputation recommended the recitation of certain portions of the Q'ran and Hadis (Muslim traditions about Prophet Mohammed) one hundred times daily for forty days. This brought no sense of relief or peace. Others changed the passages read but repeated the formula.

No improvement.

He recited one holy poem–one hundred lines long–twenty-five times nightly for forty nights while standing up to his neck in the Jhelum River in November and December, two cold months.

During this time he fasted, being allowed daily only a cup of milk and two ounces of barley.

No avail.

After three years he had exhausted the four various schools of Muslim fakirs and was no better in heart than when he began, but much poorer in pocket.

He closed his school, abandoned his duties as a maulvi and even his regular practices as a Muslim. Despite this he was, however, gaining a reputation as a particularly holy maulvi. People were increasingly coming to him for counsel and advice. He felt himself to be a deceiver. He had no right to be called maulvi sah'b when all he was was a master at duplicity and the art of deception.

To demolish his personal pride that he was seeing as the hindrance to a right relationship with God, he now praised the lowest of the Hindu castes, the Chuhras, for their qualities. He accepted food from them and earned a livelihood as peasant labor. He was desolate in spirit and wept a lot. Very occasionally he visited for private prayers a mosque or a graveyard.

He was now praying earnestly. His earlier prayer of despair, "O God, if I should die in this present condition I would surely go to hell for I have no good works to bring before you. Be merciful to me or I have no hope," he now exchanged for, "If there be such a thing as Truth, and if there be a Way, reveal it, I pray."

Mohammed Alim had no acquaintance with any Christians. These prayers were a cry from the heart of a troubled man to his God.

He now began to fear the answer to his prayer. IF God should answer it, how would he know it wasn't Iblis - Satan? He began to pray to receive an answer that should be in three distinct steps.

They were:
1. Let the answer come between two and four o'clock.
2. Let me know beforehand the appearance of the messenger you will send.
3. Let that messenger say to me, without my questioning him, "Tu Khuda ki rah ko hasil karna chahta hai?" (Do you wish to know the Way of God?)

One night, in the same year that Ditt was baptized, Muhammed Alim dreamed that a pack of dogs barred his exit from the town by the north gate. When he tried to exit by the south gate instead, the same thing happened.

The following week the dream repeated itself exactly.

A third week, the same dream was repeated but with this one variation. After trying both large gates, he remembered the wicket gate in the west wall and exited through this safely.

One week later came a different dream. In the afternoon, at four o'clock, a crowd of men stood in front of the shops on the west side of the town. In the midst of them was a man preaching the Word of God. Alim, the dreamer, remonstrated with the scoffers around the man; they shouldn't mock him, for everything he was saying was true. The man's appearance was unmistakable. He was portly in build, gray bearded, and his chapkan (coat) was peculiarly front rather than side buttoned.

The dream was so real in its detail that Mohammed Alim rose at 2 am and went at once to the location of the dream, but all was silent there.

Two more times, each a week later, this second dream was repeated without any variation.

According to the Muslim traditions of the elders, a dream repeated three times can be relied upon as coming from God.

One month after the last dream, just before four o'clock there, in front of the shops near the caravansarai, in the middle of a scoffing crowd of people was the man of the dream! It was undoubtedly he and he was preaching! His chapkan was front-buttoned!

When the crowd dispersed, the speaker went silently away into the caravansarai without saying the words Alim's prayer conditions required. This was disappointing. Alim decided to place himself "in the way." From his nearby field he plucked a bunch of millet and, striding into the caravansarai, gave it silently to one of the preacher's children. He then withdrew to his field and waited.

It was not long before Elisha Swift was standing beside him. Very quickly, with just a few searching questions and answers, Alim's background was discovered and his heart-needs answered. The stipulated words were never spoken, but instead the Way of God was quickly laid before him and made plain. The Persian

New Testament now became his most prized possession and the stimulus to all his thinking.

He was baptized in Jhelum in November of that year.

Chandu Ray and the Tibetan Lama

August 1956

Chandu Ray was the first Anglican Bishop of Karachi, appointed not too many years after Partition in the first of the sub-divisions of the great Lahore diocese that stretched from the Khyber to Karachi. He was from a Hindu background, but I am not aware of that part of his personal story. Before his appointment he had been Secretary of the Bible Society in Lahore. The Brenton Carey school and orphanage where we were living had a soft spot in his heart, for years previously he had married one of our orphanage girls. When he visited us he would sit in the window seat, open his Bible and lead an impromptu Bible study. This was a man of gentle spirit and great wisdom. The arguments within the listener subsided to acquiescence as he gently opened his heart at the prompting of Scripture, selected often at random.

How beautiful upon the mountains
Are the feet of him that bringeth
good tidings,
that publisheth peace;
Isaiah 52:7

Chandu illustrated this verse with a story from his days during the turbulence of Partition. The story is as I have held it in my memory, and it is surely recorded more accurately in some other place. Much of its details must necessarily be surmise.

It is somewhere near August 1947. He receives in Lahore, in his Bible Society office at the head of the Anarkali bazar, a telegram, unsigned. It says simply:

REVELATION 22:17,20

This reference, from the last few verses of the Bible reads:
And the Spirit and the bride say, Come,
And let everyone that heareth say, Come.

And let him that is athirst come.
And whosoever will,
let him take the water of life freely.
He which testifieth these things saith,
Surely I come quickly.

The telegram has come from the wireless telegraph station at Leh through military telegraph channels.

Leh is the most remote outpost of the old British raj proceeding up the Indus towards Tibet. The course of the Indus curls eastwards after entering the mountains and now is flowing from the east-southeast. Srinagar, the capital of Kashmir, is far to the west. To either side of the valley tower the Karakorums, many peaks over twenty thousand feet high. Highest of all is K2, Mount Godwin Austen, 28,250 feet, rising above a knot of glaciers where troops of the rival Indian and Pakistani forces are already scrambling for position in the world's highest battle ground. Leh lies on the southern slopes of the great Ladakh range a short distance north of the river.

There is no time to lose. Chandu knows exactly what the telegram is saying and from whom it has come.

Chandu has been preparing a translation of the Bible in Tibetan. The project has already taken several years. Drafts have been fully prepared in Tibetan script using Tibetans temporarily resident in India. The latest draft has been sent in its entirety back to Tibet for final review and revision. (I think, though I am not sure in my recollection, that this was being done by a Tibetan Buddhist or ex-Buddhist lama with whom Chandu had developed a close relationship. It is from this man the telegram has come.)

Obviously this man is now at Leh or nearby and is waiting for Chandu. There is no knowing how long he can wait. There is fighting at the Siachen glacier to the east of Leh already. Pakistan is still holding the bridge there.

Chandu, carrying plenty of warm clothing and a bedroll, takes the first mainline train to Taxila, changes for the railhead at Havelian, and then starts his journey by road. Up to Mansehra there are regular buses. There are jeeps now, and still a few small battered buses from Mansehra to Lari across the mountains and up to Chilas. There he catches first sight of the Indus that is to be his companion the rest of the way. It is a rushing gray, white-flecked river, already mighty, gathering momentum from the scores of rivers and rivulets feeding it from the hill clefts at either side. The time of the summer monsoon rains had, some observers felt, been deliberately chosen to dampen the fires of hatred during the partition debacle, but they hardly succeeded. Here though, virtually all are Muslim, and the anger and flames of Lahore and Amritsar are barely remarked.

Chandu skirts Nanga Parbat (the Naked Goddess) to its north side. He spends one night in Skardu, gratefully spreading his wet bedroll onto a string charpai and ignoring the bedbugs. The mountain scenery to the north is awe-inspiring. He has never seen anything like it. The world's second highest mountain towers stark and supreme, its superb slender peak struggling to reach and almost touching heaven itself. A last night in Gompa and now he is grateful for a lift from a Pakistan army jeep breaking rules to give a civilian, but a Punjabi like themselves, a ride.

At Leh, he does not head for the wooden twin cantilever bridge over the Indus but up the track towards Khardung to the north. That is where the battle line is somewhere drawn. It is from there the man he wants to meet will have come. Hardly a mile outside the town of flat-roofed timber and stone dwellings thickly clustered upon each other, soldiers stop him. They are absolutely firm. No farther. Ahead is fighting and it is no place for him or for any other civilian. Chandu looks across the bridge over the frenzied tributary and then sees, to his great joy, an old man, familiar to him, cloaked in black to his ankles, hurrying towards him from the other side. The soldiers relent. They can meet in the middle but NO FARTHER.

Chandu runs. They embrace. The other, once resident in India, breaks into Urdu/Hindi, first greetings, then news. The sack on his back he swings over his shoulder to the ground. It is Chandu's now. No opportunity for hospitality, even a cup of tea. Again they embrace. This time they are praying before parting for the last time. They will not see each other again. The task of the one is done. For him, light of load and light of heart, he will return to Khardung. A further three days steady walking will see him home.

Chandu spends that night in Leh. A first ride is available all the way to Chilas. He is keeping the sack on his lap. It is less likely to become lost there than if tucked and hidden into his bedroll. Within three days he is back in Lahore. The Bible Society staff eye his trophy almost with awe. A special room is set aside for the work. Each day that follows will start with special prayer for the completion of the task ahead.

Now to the task of publishing. Can it be done in present day Lahore? The capital of the Punjab is becoming wild and crazed. Refugees with tales of atrocities pour in from the border just thirteen miles away. Hindus flood in from the nether parts of the Punjab and the provinces to its west, hoping to escape with their lives if nothing else.

The British troops who have been trying to keep the peace have retired to their barracks. That charge now rests with the new Pakistan army, whose officers have gained promotions running ahead of their experience. They are doing their best with limited men and limited resources. The civil administration is also close to breaking. The Hindu and Sikh employees have fled for their lives, and their replacements from the ranks of the refugees will necessarily take time.

Printer's ink is not available. Chandu buys hundreds of eggs at the Tollinton market egg bazar to make his own. The paper for the Bible had arrived more than a year ago and had been in the inner store. Good quality strawboard for the hard covers is hard to find. They purchase it in dribs and drabs as they find it. The old printing presses roll. The first sheets are carefully checked. Production of the printed sheets gathers momentum. Sewing and binding is done by men and boys sitting on the floor, surrounded by an apparent chaos of papers. They are somehow retaining and, eventually, creating order. Others, standing at large tables, are gluing and fixing covers. The pace quickens as routines evolve and are improved. Steadily the pile of black volumes stacked against one wall mounts up.

The first Tibetan Bible has seen the light of day. Now to get the copies into Tibet.

Chandu explains, as he rises to leave from his window seat

at the orphanage, that when the Chinese Communist troops moved into Tibet in 1951, they gathered up all the available copies of the Tibetan Bible and used them as texts to teach the troops Tibetan.

So shall my word be
that goeth forth out of my mouth:
it shall not return unto me void,
but it shall accomplish that which I please,
and it shall prosper in the thing whereto I sent it.
Isaiah 55:11

ESTHER AT THE ORPHANAGE

June 1955

Karachi is a city built around a lagoon on the Arabian Sea that gives it a superb, sheltered harbor. It is the principal commercial and industrial center, and the only significant port for both Pakistan and for Afghanistan that has no nearer outlet to the sea. Its climate rarely exceeds one hundred degrees F in temperature but it has high humidity and, frequently, strong winds off the sea.

The Mauripur road in Karachi connected Marie's and my first home on the industrial trading estate across the mud flats to the city. In 1955 the refugees along much of its length were living in homes made out of concrete rainwater disposal pipes. The pipes were perhaps five feet in diameter and eight feet long. With burlap draped over both ends of a pipe, and hundreds of them, a whole substandard housing colony had developed. It was just one of many such colonies. The whole city was one great refugee zone. The hinterland of Karachi was desert; there were no physical limits to expansion. At the beginning of 1947 the city, beautifully clean and well ordered with wide streets and sidewalks, had had a population of about 400,000 people. By midsummer it was approaching one million, and it has gone on growing. It is now more than fourteen million.

Many of the refugees came from Southern India; their languages of Tamil and Telegu very different from the Sindhi and Urdu spoken locally. They had left all their possessions, family possessions often acquired over centuries, and had made their way either by ship from Bombay or across the desert on the narrow-gauge railway from Rajasthan. They arrived frightened and destitute in a city overwhelmed by the size of the calamity upon it.

There was one particular sanctuary of calm and tranquility right in the center of the prosperous business section of the city. Just across the road from Holy Trinity Church–a brown sandstone, Victorian Gothic garrison church–was an orphanage for girls that had been there for sixty years. Within its walls, behind the gate kept permanently locked when the gatekeeper was absent, was a little world within a world.

For most of those years, Miss Brenton Carey, a small and intrepid Englishwoman of great character and great faith, had been its guiding genius. She had come as a young woman and eventually, after more than fifty years, had died there. She, although I never met her, was to teach me several of the most important lessons of my life.

Before our marriage, Marie had encouraged me in a letter to call at the orphanage in Karachi where she had recently stayed. I should get to know her friend there, Marian Laugesen.

I am a civil engineer and was involved at that time in the construction of a cement factory in the desert. About once a month I would break away from the factory in Hyderabad to Karachi to try to get bills paid by our client. We needed that money desperately to enable us to pay our labor. I was also having some eye trouble, blurry vision and difficulty in focusing. The eye specialist refused to allow me to return to Hyderabad until massive doses of vitamins had taken effect.

This gave opportunity one day towards the end of June, as the first monsoon rains were threatening, for me to call at the orphanage. It was not difficult to find, being on the main road between the city and the cantonment.

Marian, a bright, bustling and cheerful New Zealander, had been hostess to Marie just six months previously when the Laubach Team had been demonstrating "Each One Teach One" to literacy experts and teachers.

She welcomed me and invited me, before having tea with her, to see around the orphanage. I had never been in an orphanage before. It was afternoon. It was rest time, the school was over for the day, and the day children had gone home. It was a very different world to the world I knew outside its walls. It was a female world, almost. There were fifty-three girls and one boy, a brother who could not be separated from his sister. There were several elderly or mentally infirm women who were also under Marian's care.

I paused suddenly. A girl, a girl in perhaps her mid-twenties, was sitting on the edge of the verandah, leaning against one of the sandstone columns. She was feeding with a bottle an infant child. She was an Indian girl, wearing a red sari rather than the more familiar shalwarqamiz. She looked up as we approached and smiled. She was, simply, the most beautiful woman I'd ever seen. Her complexion was slightly darker than the Punjabi complexion to which I was accustomed. Her jet-black hair was brushed straight back and gathered into braids. Coupled with the perfect oval of the Indian feature and her youth was something more. She had an inner glow of tranquility that seemed to shine out of her into the air around and enhance it with the perfume of her presence. I was only to see her once again, in very similar circumstances eight hundred miles distant from Karachi, but I was never to forget her.

Men were rare at the orphanage but, accompanied by Marian, I was obviously no stranger but a friend. A few words were exchanged, a parting smile and then, as we moved on, I asked Marian who that lovely girl was.

"Oh, that's Esther," and then, over tea, she explained.

Esther had come with her family not long after Partition. They were Muslim as almost all refugees were, and they came from South India.

In 1946, Esther had changed school from a government school to attend a mission school at Madras. It was the year before the partition of India into India and Pakistan. She was a quiet shy girl who talked little, but this change gave her opportunity to grow into a new enlarged world with much broader spiritual boundaries than those possessed by her friends, boundaries they had not even dreamed of. She seemed to have found a bridge. She shared nothing of what she was experiencing with her parents or her large family of brothers and sisters. She confided only with Miss Christian, her teacher.

She treasured her Bible. She could leave it at school. The questions that arose in her mind she took to her teacher, an Indian woman who exemplified to her all the true Christian graces. The answers she received satisfied her. Although she was Muslim in a Christian mission school it was Esther, then known as Qamar, who now regularly began to win the Scripture prizes. One of them was a New Testament small enough to be easily hidden in her clothing.

Before the upheaval of leaving home and friends and mentors at school, this book had spoken with increasing compulsion to her heart. She read it through again, and by the time to depart forever from her birthplace, she was reading it through yet again. She went back to certain special passages frequently. Something strange was happening to her. Through this book she was finding the reality of the Christian experience of God.

In her heart she was now no longer Muslim, for she had committed herself to the One who had said, "I am the Way, the Truth and the Life, no one cometh unto the Father but by me."

She did not feel she could safely bring her treasured Bible with her to Pakistan although she hated parting with it. She asked her teacher to keep it for her until, God willing, she was able to retrieve it.

On her way, somewhere, she didn't know where, her New Testament, her dearest treasure, fell from her clothes and was lost. She repeated to herself whatever she could remember. She had no contact with Christians, just memories of those she had left behind in Madras who had befriended her. The family settled, like many other refugees, in the slum colony of Lyari in Karachi. Several of her brothers found work. Her father died.

Marian smiled thoughtfully as she recounted Esther's story.

"I received one day, while the refugees were still pouring in, a letter from an Indian Christian teacher in Madras who had been provided my name and address by local missionaries. A girl in whom she was interested, Qamar Ziai, had written to her. She was now living in Lyari. Would I go to visit her?

"Eventually, after walking along many dusty alleys and searching refugee colonies, one morning I found her. She was living in a hut, like so many others, where the walls were pieces of burlap sacking stretched between light wooden frame supports. There was a lovely mother, and with her several of her family of sons and daughters. Among them was Qamar, Esther. Like you I was struck by her beauty.

"When the older women went out to prepare tea for their unexpected guest, Esther quickly leaned over and whispered to me, 'I don't have a Bible, please bring me a New Testament.' I nodded.

"Two weeks later I visited again. Esther asked me to teach her some English, brought some schoolbooks and gave them to me. Inside one of them she quickly hid the New Testament.

"I would occasionally visit her. I had given her my address, but then I was transferred from Karachi and lost touch with her. Occasionally when I remembered her I prayed for her.

"Four years ago I returned here to the Orphanage, but even in that short time, Karachi had doubled in size. Many of the refugee colonies had by now grown into shantytowns. Some had even been made pukka (well-built). I didn't try to find her although naturally I wondered what had happened to her.

"Then, hardly a fortnight ago, Esther turned up here. The young girl had turned into the lovely mature woman you have just seen. She was distraught. I brought her in and gave her some tea. She told me of her faithful loneliness. Other than me, she had not had contact with any Christian for eight years; now she had left her home and come to us. She had resisted being forced into an unwilling marriage. She had read her New Testament over and over and over again. She had memorized many passages.

"She is sharing a bedroom with two of the school teachers who have befriended her. Janebai and Miss Jhaga Mall and I have been giving her the Christian fellowship and support she has been starved for over these many years–it has been such a joy to be able to encourage her understanding and respond to her questions. They are not superficial; they show great depth of understanding. Together we chose her new name, Esther John. I've been spending time with her every day, reading and praying. Now she has a full Bible rather than just the New Testament, so there is a lot of catching up to do."

I asked Marian whether there had been any contact from her family.

"Yes, we thought we had lost her. When she had been here just five days, Jugenoo, her youngest brother, a favorite of hers, turned up. They had been so worried about her. They didn't know what had happened to her. She was very sorry for their concern but said she would remain here. Her mother could come here to see her and she would like to see her.

"Instead, several days later, Jugenoo brought only an older brother. While I was talking to him Jugenoo told Esther, speaking Tamil, that her mother was ill. Did she not care for her mother? With some hesitation Esther took her bus fare and some rupees and went with them, promising to be back the following day.

"She did not return."

It was easy to follow what had happened. Now that they had got Esther back home, she was not to be given opportunity to slip away. Her oldest brother, acting in place of her father, expressed the family's anger at her action. The family lived in a concrete-block house. Rooms could be secured and one of the brothers was always close by. Time to speed up the business of marrying Esther. Many of the lengthy preparations would need to be set aside.

Esther was beautiful. There was little difficulty in finding widowers who were wealthy, younger men with prospects and good family, and many others with less prospects. Quickly the suitors were whittled down. Esther was not consulted, but the whole family wanted to make sure that her husband should be principled, firm in the faith, secure in his prospects and of good family and reputation. Soon, a couple of days of intense conversations and they were ready to make the announcement. All had been agreed upon between the two families. The young man was reasonably good looking which was a bonus. The families were gathering even though there was a bus strike and riots in the city.

Alarm, Esther was missing!

She had, without rousing anyone's suspicion, slipped away from visiting at a neighbor's house and without going home, had caught a cycle rickshaw from Lyari as far as Empress Market. There was rioting in the streets there; buses were being stoned and burned, people were getting hurt and the police, armed with brass tipped staffs, were swinging about them. She skirted the crowds and hurried up through the back streets of the Elphinstone bazar, cut through into the main street, moderated her pace to that of the sauntering crowd and crossed over into Bonus Road. The watchman opened the gate when she rattled it urgently, wanting to call out, "Hurry, please, hurry!" as he sauntered up from his shade under the great peepul tree. She exchanged few words with him. He was old and grizzled and kindly, but he was a Muslim. He took her up to the big room and called Marian to tell her Esther was back.

There had been almost continuous prayer for Esther by the whole orphanage family. Into the early hours of each morning the staff had been in prayer.

What was going to happen now, I asked. The family knew where she was most likely to be.

Sosan, the teacher, was having to go back to the Punjab on the night train tonight. Her mother was seriously ill. Esther would go with her. They would be leaving for the cantonment station in an hour or so. Hopefully no one would come before then.

Esther At Gujranwala

March 1958

Marian Peterson was principal of the United Bible Training Center in Gujranwala. She was a lovely, gentle, elderly American I had taken to immediately on meeting her. She had asked if I would call in on my journey home from Lahore to advise her on a building problem. She needed more accommodation for her women students. For security reasons the center had been designed around a small quadrangle with verandahs abutting it. Behind the verandahs were the perimeter rooms, classroom, chapel, dormitory, office and staff rooms and stores. An intruder would have to climb high walls onto the roof to enter.

It was afternoon when I called. I wondered whether Marian would be resting. She was not. When I rang the bell at the corner entrance, she answered the door and invited me in. The bamboo curtains known as "chicks" had not yet been unrolled to shade the verandah, although by now the afternoon sun was warm.

All of Marian's students were resting, or, rather, almost all of them. Marian had been sitting in a low cane bottomed chair on the edge of the verandah with a student seated opposite her leaning against one of the brick columns. They had obviously been having some additional study together, for both had books open before them.

I caught a glimpse of the girl student and caught my breath at the same time. I had seen that same unforgettable girl before, three years previously and eight hundred miles away. Then too, she had been sitting on a verandah but at that time holding and feeding an infant child from a bottle. Her beauty was as striking as it had been then in the orphanage, taking root and fullness from within. She gave me a smile as she excused herself so that Marian could deal with me. I was not to see her again.

Marian explained Esther to me. Originally she was from South India. She had come to Christ herself through reading the New Testament privately.

Because she had not been born Christian, she was absorbing what she was taught like a sponge and could not get enough nourishment. It was a joy to be teaching her, for her questions indicated a freshness of inquiry, and at the same time a maturity of perception that was an exhilarating combination. Rarely had Marian enjoyed a student so much.

She would complete her training as a Bible woman, and then there would have to be great care where she was placed to work. She had no relatives who would be caring for her or to whom she could go for festivals or holidays. Possibly she might go to one of the Mission hospitals alongside a senior Bible Woman who would be her mentor and protector. Possibly too, she might go with some single missionary women (missahibas) working in the rural districts of the Punjab or perhaps, even better, with a missionary family in district work who would make her part of the family. No, Marian did not think her own family had any idea where she was. She received very few letters.

Esther At Chichawatni

Spring 1960

Esther had lived in institutions ever since she left her Karachi home almost five years ago in June. Her favorite home among them all was the nurses hostel at the hospital in Montgomery (now known as Sahiwal). It was there that she had asked to be baptized. There her Christian family had developed. It was there that her new family sought, with her concurrence, to find a suitable husband for her although no arrangement matured. To them also she returned on her holidays from the Bible Training Center in Gujranwala and after her two visits home to her family in Karachi.

These journeys home had been taken with trepidation, but at the urging of much inner love for her mother and for her brothers and sisters and now, the young nieces and nephews also. They were journeys guarded with much Punjabi prayer. Her Montgomery family could not rest easy until she was back. Among her family in Karachi she had been received lovingly. No undue pressure was put upon her, although again she was asked whether she was yet ready for a marriage arrangement. Marian was no longer at the orphanage, but each time she called in to see how her baby charges had grown, and to be remembered and to tell her story.

In April 1959, Dale and Janet White, the buzurgs (elders) of the Associate Reformed Presbyterian Mission, sister mission to the Sialkot Mission, moved from Montgomery thirty miles west to Chichawatni, along the main railway line to Karachi. Chichawatni had been their first home nearly forty years previously. It was to Janet that Marian Laugesen had sent Esther and Sosan. Janet had been born in the country, the daughter of missionary parents. She was Esther's Punjabi "mother" and spoke Punjabi far better than this particular daughter was ever able to speak it.

Janet, soon after settling in and meditating on the meaning of "Every one of you that has two coats give to him that has none," asked to be shown what that was to mean to her. The answer came immediately, "Invite Esther here and give her your guest room."

Janet was a dutiful missionary wife. She knew that hospitality was an inevitable part of those duties. She had no other guest room, but no matter.

Esther was delighted to have a room of her own. This was hers. This was something that belonged to her. On the back porch a small kitchen was built for her. Now she could cook those hot Madrasi curries to her heart's content. She loved flowers and decorated her room with them. She set her few belongings to decorate her room as attractively as she could. At Gujranwala she had learned to ride a bicycle, and she garaged her bicycle on the back porch.

She was now working with Janet as a woman evangelist (the local term was "Bible woman"), and sometimes teaching not only Bible but also literacy in her excruciating distortion of a Punjabi dialect. The two women would go out on their bicycles along the rutted village tracks where Janet was already well known. Esther, as her companion and with her own winning characteristics, was soon as welcome as Janet.

That winter was one of the happiest in Esther's life. Winter was tent time for district missionaries like the Whites. Tents would be set up on the edge of a village for maybe a week of meetings before moving to another location. Esther had her own very patched and worn tent. She loved her tent and shared it with a visiting Christian nurse from the hospital who ran her dispensary alongside Esther's Bible and literacy teaching with Janet. The nurses changed week by week, but the intention always was that Esther not be alone.

Visitors from Chichawatni brought out the mail for the itinerating camp. During the fall season of touring around the district, Esther received several letters from Karachi in addition to those from her growing Punjabi family and friends. Jugenoo was soon to be married and likely too to move to another house. Mother wasn't looking forward to being alone. When was Qamar going to come home to visit?

She made up her mind. They all would go back to Chichawatni for Christmas. Esther planned to do a Christmas drama with the children, and then after Christmas, she would go home once more to Karachi to see the family.

She had already packed her trunk. She had acquired a few gifts to take with her but she was uneasy. Four times already her brothers had made arrangements for her marriage even though she had made her opposition plain. She prayed about it into the New Year and then wrote home. She would come home to visit them IF they would allow her to live as a Christian AND not try to force her into a marriage not of her own choosing. She registered the letter to ensure its delivery.

No answer ever came.

The spring tent tour was half way through. It was the end of January. The time had been good. There would be a short break back at the house for the monthly pastor's meeting, and then to a final location for the tail end of winter before it became too hot. Already they were noticing the days were getting warmer although they still used shawls in the evening. At the house, as soon as they returned, Janet got on with the preparations for her twenty guests. She recovered from the steel drums the quilts and blankets and pillows, and gave to the cook rice, flour, spices and money to buy meat.

Late afternoon she took Esther a glass of the buffalo milk the villagers had sent with them when they left. The young woman was happy to be home, dusting everything, polishing her pots and pans, setting her vase of flowers, and singing to herself. She would go to bed early. She would fall asleep to the sound of the chimta (firetongs) and dholki and harmonium and the Psalms that were the hymnody of the rural church.

It is unlikely she awoke again after she fell asleep. How her assailant entered no one knew. She was discovered dead the following morning, struck twice, brutally and bloodily on the head with some heavy, sharp instrument.

Inquiries revealed that a man, certainly not Punjabi or Pathan, had been inquiring for her. The police failed to conclude their investigations as to the identity of her assailant. Suspicions that it was a member of her family were never proven.

In Britain during the summer of 1998, ten empty niches on the great west front of Westminster Abbey, the nation's most visited church, were filled with the statues of contemporary martyrs. The niches had stood empty since the Abbey was built in the eleventh century. They were unveiled by the Queen just before the Lambeth Conference of Anglican bishops led by the Archbishop of Canterbury. Representative bishops from all over the world were present.

One of the ten statues is that of Esther John.

The Blind Afghan

June 1973

Zaid is not one of the beggars in Betty Wilson's blind school in Kabul, but he too is blind. He comes from a different level in society but sometimes sits with the others as they weave baskets and talk. He is well educated and has a questioning mind. In particular he never tires of probing Betty's faith. Why does she believe what she does? How does she know the Bible is a reliable record? How does what she believes affect what she is doing? Why is she here in Kabul anyway? Surely there is work for her husband back in America. Can he also weave baskets? Who pays him? Is it the American Government?

Zaid's mind is alert and intelligent. He remembers Betty's answers and sometimes, when Betty is absent, plays devil's advocate in conversation with the others.

Almost indiscernibly something is happening to the man. When he goes back into the outside world, he is tempering his language with kindness, accepting rebuffs with a smile.

Caught by surprise and a strange joy that seems to bring light into the darkness of his blind world, he is now declaring what his heart is telling him is simply the incredible staggering truth– *for God so loved the world that He gave his only begotten Son that whosoever believeth on him shall not perish but have everlasting life.* He is declaring this in what are possibly the most dangerous bazars in the world for a declaration of the Gospel.

Zaid is fearless. His very blindness gives him courage a sighted man would lack. He cannot see the looks thrown angrily at him, the tapping of the forehead to tell that he is mad and simply to be disregarded. He senses the discord his remarks arouse and is simply roused to more zeal. The mind of a blind man, without the allurements and distractions that sight brings, feeds on noises and voices.

He will nurse a response into a conversation, a conversation into a discussion and a discussion into an argument. There he is wonderfully at home. He knows the Q'ran Sharif well and uses it readily to refute objections. The maulvis cannot force him to back down. He knows better than most of them what their Holy Book says. Raised voices in protest and anger are food to his soul. Who would strike a blind man?

In midsummer, trouble erupts as within a few days the completed church being built alongside the blind school is demolished under government orders. International protests only trigger further reaction. The school for the blind is to be closed immediately. The Christy Wilsons are expelled on short notice.

Zaid continues boldly in his witness in Kabul but eventually, after the Russians have moved in and the guerrilla warfare against them starts in earnest, he too, with his family (his wife also is blind but retains a little sight) makes his way to Torkham and crosses the border into Pakistan. In the refugee camp that lies between Jamrud and Peshawar, his zeal is unabated.

One day he disappears. The American Ambassador appeals to Gulbuddin Hekmatyar, leader of the fighters against the Russians, that this blind man not be harmed.

No firm news of him surfaces to tell how he died, but gradually reports emerge and seem supported from different sources. What follows must be at least partially surmise.

He is kept in captivity for two years by the Mujahideen (Afghan guerrillas) and moved about from camp to camp within Pakistan. Finally he is taken across the North Waziristan border to Khost in Afghanistan.

One day he is brought out before a powerful guerrilla leader noted for his Islamic zeal. "Recite the kalma!" comes the order. The kalma is the simple affirmation of the Muslim faith. Silence. The order is repeated. Again silence.

There is no one present to offer Zaid words of courage or counsel. He is alone. Alone in his own sightless world. Alone among his own countrymen. Alone among enemies. They are all his enemies. Enemies because he chooses, because he is constrained to believe differently to the way they believe. He senses the crisis his silence creates. The tension mounts. He cannot speak, he just cannot. His mind, his heart, will not allow him to. Someone, someone unknown to him, merely a voice, not an interrogator, not an enemy, almost, by the softness of his tone a neutral even if not a friend, urges him to comply. He cannot do so.

Now, for a last time, the order is given. "Recite the kalma." He remains silent.

The next order is different. "Put out your tongue." A blow across the back of his head. He puts out his tongue. His head jerks forward as his tongue is seized and pulled and then slashed. Searing agonizing pain!! It is the end.

His tongue has been cut off. For three days he lies dying. That merciful release is speeded by a contemptuous bullet in the stomach from the man who had wielded the knife.

In Canterbury Cathedral near my home, at the east end in the corona is the chapel of modern martyrs. Great men and women, Bonhoeffer, Edith Stein, Dehqani-Tafti are remembered there. The twentieth century, the century of enlightenment, of the airplane and the computer, has seen more Christian martyrs than any other century. Some are known. Many more are unknown and unrecorded on any page of history. The new century promises to be little better.

DR. RAZZAQ AND THE QADIANIS

May 31, 1974

This story is somewhat at odds with the others, but it deserves its place in a chronicle of courage. Since the terrorist attack on September 11th in New York it has been easy to demonize Islam as the heart source of international terrorism.

It is not like that at all. My personal journeys brought me into touch with many men and women of Muslim faith who became, and are, close and valued friends. All faiths have extremists, but their extremism or the extent of their violence does not make them representative or typical or permit blanket judgment. It is the present Pakistan president who declares with courage that the greatest threat to his Islamic state is Muslim extremism. He is committed to fight it, and so are many others about whom we will not hear. This tells an earlier story.

When I returned to Pakistan in 1953, martial law was imposed as a consequence of violent communal riots against a small but zealous Islamic group known variously as Qadianis, Ahmadiyas and Mirzais. The riots cost many lives.

The Ahmadiya sect of Islam was founded by Mirza Ghulam Ahmad at the turn of the twentieth century. He was an Indian Muslim who began from his home village of Qadian in the Punjab. Initially he was writing books against the Christian missionaries in defense of Islam, but in 1879 he added the claim that he was the promised Mahdi and the Messiah. Over against a general Muslim belief that Jesus was not actually crucified but was raised to heaven and will reappear on earth, Mirza claimed that Jesus, after escaping crucifixion, went to Kashmir and died in Srinagar. He also claimed to be a later manifestation of Mohammed the Prophet and for the Hindus the Incarnation of Krishna. He accepted the Q'ran and Islamic Law. In Pakistan, where the movement now has its headquarters at Rabwah, believers declare that all those Muslims who do not believe in Mirza Ghulam Ahmad are unbelievers.

Kenneth Old

31.5.74

Down in the town men died today,
Pitched from the roofs of their homes
By the men who were their neighbors,
Whose buffaloes gave them their milk
And whose children played together.
Some had their eyes gouged out by claws
That hours before were gentle hands
Engaged in soft caresses.
Children had their tongues cut out
Struggling in terror while around
Invective in the name of God
Profaned the air they gulped
In screams reduced to a whimper.
In Qila Didar Singh a man was
Stabbed and hacked to little pieces
By friends with whom he'd shared
Just yesterday the wooden plough.
Houses smoldered through the night.
At last the firing died away.
Later,
The mosques were full in curfew time
With men making obeisance now
Dishonor had been assuaged
And the Precious Name of God
Been defended and acquitted.
–Only here and there the whisper breaks
Upon the silence 'We are mad, we are mad!'

A couple of hundred yards down the Sialkot Road towards the city, a family of Qadianis has come running into the garden of Dr. Razzaq. He has been a medical officer in Burma during the war, assigned to a British unit. He saved one British soldier's life by swimming across a river in flood with the man on his back and the

Japanese not far behind. He is no stranger to danger and does not lack courage.

The panic stricken and desperate people are strangers to him. He invites them in. He seats them. He has been hearing for some hours the spasmodic firing from the city and from the housing colony to the rear of his house. He knows they have gone mad in the city.

The family is fleeing from a mob pursuing them. There is hardly time even to explain, no time even to exchange names. The mob has burst in past the iron gates into the garden. The bell rings, violently and urgently. Dr. Razzaq looks out of the window. He goes to his cupboard and takes out his .45 pistol, checks that each of the six chambers is full, releases the safety catch and cocks the trigger. He opens the door. The leaders of the mob have retreated to the foot of the steps. With the gun he waves them back farther. He pulls the door closed behind him.

"Dr. Sah'b, please send the Qadianis out. We'll take them outside; we won't do anything here."

"Why do you want them, have they done something wrong?"

"They are Qadianis, Dr. Sah'b, they are blasphemers."

"Gentlemen, you know me. I am a Muslim, a Sunni Muslim. Have you anything against me?"

"No, Sah'b, nothing at all. You are our doctor."

"Then let me tell you something. I wonder if my faith is different from yours. For MY faith requires me to give hospitality to strangers and these people ARE MY GUESTS!"

His voice is raised now and the pistol, unwavering, is aimed at the mob spokesman who is responding to him.

"These people you want are my guests and I defend them with my own life! In this gun are six bullets. Six men among you will die before you mount these steps. I shall not miss!"

There is a moment's silence broken only by the sound of continuing firing from beyond the railway station. He speaks once more.

"YOU are not my guests and I have not invited you onto my property. You are trespassing. Any man who is here in one minute, his life is forfeit to me. GO!!"

They go. They go even faster than they came in. He slowly walks down the steps and puts the chain around the gate and padlocks it. The mob is streaming back to the city to find other victims. He goes in and offers his guests tea.

Excerpt from KGO letter dated June 1st, 1974

Shops and houses smolder in the town. Along the Grand Trunk Road angry crowds stop vehicles and compliant travelers shout "Mirzai dogs!" before they can continue. A Pathan tribesman tells Ken, "You Christians and we Muslims are brothers but these Mirzais - (spit)! In the town nine of them . . ." and he draws his finger across his throat in an act of finality. Many bodies, mutilated, burned or shot, are reported in the hospital along the road. More lie under the ashes of their burned homes. The Mirzai mosque is burned. A curfew is declared. Stories filter in of men stabbed and quartered, of others clubbed to death or flung from their own roofs to their death, of some with eyes gouged out, of children with tongues cut out, of desperate gun battles as terrified men folk hold off arsonists.

Our Muslim friends despairingly say, "A madness is upon us, it is like 1947 over again and we are doing it to ourselves!"

What is it all about?

Medical students laughed insults as they passed through Rabwah on their way north by special train. Rabwah is the town in the desert between Sargodha and the river Chenab created by immigrants from Qadian in India. The Qadianis are an industrious tithing missionary-minded people perhaps analogous to Jehovah's Witnesses. When the train returned on its way back south they were met by a crowd of five thousand angry Mirzais who beat them up.

Now all of Pakistan seems involved in retaliation. There is a complete blackout on what is happening but the church elders who met in our living room this morning to discuss congregational matters are gravely aware of the implication of these events for another minority community, their own.

Excerpt from KGO letter
November 12th, 1974

This summer there was public rioting and murder against members of the Mirzai sect culminating in a declaration by the National Assembly that there has been no prophet subsequent to Mohammed and that therefore the Mirzais are not Muslims.

There, that should take care of it!

Gulsher

It is a month after spring admissions and the technical school in Gujranwala is full. We have taken in more boys than ever before. Our initial planning had been for 250 and had we ever erred! Most of my mistakes, and there were a great many, I could put down to having a very minimal vision of what should and could be.

A pastor I know slightly brings into the office a young man in his late twenties. He wants me to admit him. I am brusque and impolite. The school is full and the young man is over age. We have placed an upper age limit of twenty-one, and he must be nearly thirty. The two follow me as I hurry off to give a surveying lesson. "Yes, he may well be a special case but we have completed our admissions, and even if he had been here at that time I would not have admitted him. He is too old. I am sorry, there is no question of admission!"

They turn away at the drafting shop door, deeply disappointed.

During the evening, thinking back over the day, I am ashamed of my behavior. I had been deeply discourteous. I walk back over to the office and search for the admission application. Yes, there it is; the boy's, no, man's photograph is attached to it. Gulsher Inayat. It gives the home address, a village outside Gujrat some thirty-five miles away.

I write a letter of apology. It had been my duty to hear the reasons he wanted to put forward why he should be an exception. I had not allowed him to do so. I had done wrong and I regretted it. If he wished to come and see me, no need to bother the pastor who had brought him, I would see him and hear his story but, as I had explained, there could be little hope of admission.

Several days later Gulsher arrived alone. As I took him into the staff room to talk, before he could say anything, I apologized for my rudeness to him. He seemed surprised. What was I making a fuss about? He had known I would call him back. He had not been at all worried. Had not God told him to come here? Was God ever wrong?

He told me his story. I think we talked in Urdu but possibly it was in English. He had been a Muslim until recently.

"I come from a wealthy landowning family. We have many fields. My father was anxious for me to get a good education. After high school I attended the local government college. I went in by bus every day. My favorite subjects were English literature and English language. I loved debating. Some of the most interesting debates were not in the college at all but down at the mosque. A bunch of us would go down at lunch break and bait the maulvi. Many of us knew more Arabic than he did. We would argue over the Q'ran, over Qadianis, over women's rights, over Shariat law, over anything that he mentioned. What he favored we opposed, what he opposed we favored.

"To get us off his back he would attack the Christians and we, I, would defend them. He raised questions though about them and I didn't know the answers. I wasn't going to let him get the upper hand over me. There was a Bible Institute based in one of the old missionary bungalows in the town. I'd seen the sign. I listed the questions I needed answered and went along there after college one afternoon. I met the principal–he was a Pakistani or maybe an Indian–explained what I needed, and asked him if he could let me have the answers if I called in next morning on my way to college.

"We covered many things about Christians in the next few months: why they behave so badly if what they believe is so good; whether the New Testament about Jesus, and Mohammed, has been altered; whether the Bible is really the Word of God; who Jesus really is, whether he really did die on the cross. Many of the answers came from the Q'ran itself. I didn't realize what was happening. I was getting an education about two faiths, my own and the Christian faith. Something was stirring in my own heart that had less and less to do with the debates and the maulvi. Soon I gave up going down to the Mosque, but I kept going to my new friends with questions of my own.

"I was working through things myself, finding myself less and less in touch with the interests of my friends in college. I had come to believe that what the Christians believed was true, but I was afraid of what would happen should my family ever hear of it. I was very careful to give them no clue, but more and more I was being constrained inwardly to go one step further, the one step further and be baptized. I wondered whether I could just be a secret Christian. After all, the Christians in Gujrat were mostly sweepers, and mine was a high family.

"One day, I was baptized. In a canal. I had done it! Just a few were there. They would not say anything until they heard that I myself had spoken out. I walked home as though I was walking on air. There was such a great sense of freedom and joy. I sneaked upstairs to my room. No one saw me. I knelt down and prayed to God in Jesus' name.

"My family must have seen something had happened to me when I came down, for I was so happy but I did not tell them. That night I had a dream.

"I dreamt I saw Jesus coming across the field toward me. He came up so close we could touch each other. There was such love on His face. He said 'Gulsher, today you were baptized with water, but I want you to be baptized in the Holy Spirit. Before that happens, something has to die.' I looked down. There was a bed just beside me and on it lay a body, the body of a dead man. I looked more closely. I recognized the man. It was me!

"I looked back at Jesus. He stretched out his arms and wrapped them closely around me, tight and yet tighter and tighter. There was no resistance of body against body and I realized, with immense flooding joy, that we were merging into each other; that I was in Him and He was in me. That's what the Bible says, isn't it? *Christ in me, the Hope of Glory!*

"And then I awoke. I knew who my Hope of Glory was.

"My parents know now and I have had to leave home, but God has sent me here."

Over the years I occasionally ran into Gulsher after he completed his draftsman course. He was usually out of jail on bail or waiting to go back in. All kinds of false charges were brought against him, including one of murder. I do not think that Gulsher was married when I first met him, although he might have been.

Some years after he graduated, he came in to see me with an invitation to visit. Marie and I and a couple of our young volunteers drove to his village home late one afternoon. He showed us the fields, the private irrigation canals, the water garden where the women walked in the cool of the evening. He could not invite us into the house. His parents would object. He regretted this. We were his guests and he the host, so he was ashamed for this omission. Instead he insisted, with apologies, on buying us all Coca Colas at the roadside stall before we left for home.

I last met him in Lahore just before his court hearing on an attempted murder charge. His wife, a cousin relative, was valiantly trying to help him defend himself against the charges against him. I do not know what happened.

Kalim - Outward Journey

Kalim is not his real name. It is a name he chose later. He is not prepossessing to look at; a rather short man, early middle age, stocky build, thinning black hair, a pockmarked rather chubby face. He wears brown shalwarqamiz and dark glasses. He has just been speaking to our boys in the early morning chapel. He has spoken an accented guttural Urdu, clearly not his native tongue. He has held them spellbound. You could have heard a pin drop.

We walk over to the house for a cup of tea, and I try to get inside the mind of this man and understand his thinking. His story is going round and round in my thoughts. I have reconstructed it below.

Kalim is a Pathan. He actually lives within the Khyber Pass linking the Peshawar plain to the Afghan border, so he is likely an Afridi. The thirty-three mile long pass has many small high-walled settlements. Each has its own familiar yet peculiar mud plastered watchtower at one corner overlooking the gate through the wall.

He has had a good education, finishing at the University between Jamrud and Peshawar. He specialized in Arabic. Now he works at the Peshawar station of Radio Pakistan. He is not a top-flight announcer but he fills in as needed and broadcasts the regular early morning prayers. This has so pleased his parents, who are staunch in their faith and commitment.

One of the five pillars of Islam is the performance, once in a lifetime, of the pilgrimage to Mecca. Kalim resolves not to wait until he is an old man; he will go now. Not only his father but the neighbors are happy to help finance his journey. There are a number of ways to get to Mecca from where he lives. The wealthy fly; thousands who are fortunate in the draw go on the haj ship 'Saffina ul Hajjaz' from Karachi. He will take the least expensive way, overland through Afghanistan, Iran, Kuwait and then down the coast of the Persian Gulf to Dammam before the final overland stage of the journey. It will be an interesting experience to see

Kenneth Old

these lands along the way.

Whole parties of Pathans are traveling together. The journey is enlivened by the excitement of anticipation. Several buses are traveling in a group, and amongst the passengers are imams, maulvis and street-side vehicle mechanics who are quite accustomed to fixing buses by the roadside. The buses stop for prayers at the regular times and a glance at the sun confirms the direction of Mecca. There are regular caravansarais along the way where beds can be rented. Just as often as not, the buses drive on through the night.

From Dammam it is now west across the last desert, through Riyadh, and then up across the brown hills of the low plateau. At last, Afif long past, they glimpse Taif and finally, through the pass and distant in the evening haze, they glimpse the holy city itself. They have arrived!

The experience of the Hajj (pilgrimage to Mecca) is simply the most awe-inspiring event that Kalim has ever experienced. It has far more impact upon him than he imagined in his wildest dreams. It is not only the immense concourse of people - black people, brown people like himself, even a few white people, Asiatics, Aryans, Africans. It seems as though the followers of the Prophet come from all parts of the whole wide world. All wear similar simple white vestments. It is not his induction into an annual tradition going back fourteen centuries. It is not the sense of unity he finds with strangers he will only ever meet here. It is the sense of God! He is thinking deeper about God than he has ever thought in his life. God is a reality to be touched and felt! Can he hold on to this when he returns home to Khyber?

The journey back is not, strangely, anticlimactic. The passengers carry a different sense of excitement. Anticipation has been replaced by consummation, and with the consummation has come awe. For all who journey, a lifetime's dream is replaced with thankfulness and a sense of the worldwide reach of their faith.

The buses divert into Bahrein for the night. This will be the place where many of the new hajjis (Mecca pilgrims) will pick up gifts, mementos and personal items before they turn north to head across Iran to Mashhad. Kalim turns unwisely down a poorly lighted alley linking two main streets.

His eyes open. He blinks. Where is he? He closes his eyes again. His head is throbbing. He is in a bed. His head is bandaged and the bandages are tight. Various parts of his body, his ribs, and his legs hurt. He stretches his fingers, tries to wriggle his toes. Something has happened. What has happened? Where was he last? He remembers saying to another passenger that he would cut through to the other street where they said the radios were. He remembers the sound of footsteps hurrying behind him but he pays no attention to them. He remembers nothing further. His head hurts so! He is so dry! His mouth feels like caked desert mud, cracked and parched. He croaks "water, water." His voice sounds odd to his ears. A wet cloth is passed across his lips. Such relief! He takes an end into his mouth and sucks it. He opens his eyes. Bending over him is an elderly woman. He does not know her but her eyes are caring and her face filled with compassion. She holds the wet cloth to his lips. She calls out and another younger woman and an elderly man join her. They are excited, talking in Arabic. He can understand! Thank God! "Where am I?" Can that be his voice?

The man does not answer but kneels beside him and, placing an arm behind it, lifts the pillow and Kalim's head. Ouch! The young woman is holding a metal beaker to his lips. He gulps. Nectar! He almost empties the beaker but they remove it. His eyes are darting around the room trying to work out his surroundings. "Where am I?" The curtains are pulled across to darken the room and the surroundings are indistinct.

The man speaks slowly. "You are in Bahrein. We live here. Our family name is Sadiq; my name is Haroon Sadiq. I found you in the alley when I came home from work four days ago. My daughter and I brought you inside. We were afraid you were going to die but we didn't want to move you. My wife has been looking after you. The doctor has been here, and now that you are conscious we will call him again. What is your name? What country are you from? Do you have any friends here?"

The first few details exchanged, Kalim closes his eyes. The curtains are pulled back just a little, the visitors tiptoe away, and he sleeps again.

The ensuing days, then weeks, see a slow but gradual improvement in Kalim's condition. The gaping wound on his head heals to a scar, the bruises disappear, and his difficult, crippled walk improves to a hobble and then a limp. No bones are actually broken. All that Kalim possesses are his clothes he was found in. His body belt containing his money and his passport are gone. As soon as he is able, he reports to the Pakistan consulate in Bahrein. He is issued temporary travel documents to get back home.

The Sadiq family is Christian. They do not seem disturbed by the fact their involuntary guest is a Muslim. He wonders why they are helping him. He is and has been a considerable expense to them and much trouble. They treat him as one of the family and are concerned for him. He joins as an observer in their family devotions. They read to him from their Injil a story told by Jesus.

A certain man went down from Jerusalem to Jericho,
and fell among thieves,
which stripped him of his raiment,
and wounded him
and departed, leaving him half dead.
And by chance there came down a certain priest that way;
and when he saw him, he passed by on the other side.
And likewise a Levite, when he was at the place,
came and looked on him, and passed by on the other side.
But a certain Samaritan, as he journeyed,
came where he was:
and when he saw him, he had compassion on him.
And went to him, and bound up his wounds,
pouring in oil and wine,
and set him on his own beast,
and brought him to an inn,
and took care of him.
Luke 10:30–34

Kalim looks around at their smiling faces. These people, strangers, actually love him. How incredible! He has done nothing to deserve it and yet they love him. What kind of love is this?

When Kalim leaves them to resume his journey home by a series of regular bus journeys across several countries, he takes with him the assurance of the Sadiq's prayers and the memories of a personal disaster retrieved by kindness into blessing. He takes with him also two gifts. One is a gift of money to get him to his own door, and the other is an Arabic New Testament.

Kalim - Homecoming

As he journeys, the New Testament becomes for Kalim his focused interest. Prompted initially by a desire to explain to himself what has motivated his host family to help him, he soon becomes caught up instead in a search for the real Jesus. Jesus was a prophet; that he well knows. Jesus in character and gifts was unique. The Q'ran Sharif praises him.

The Injil paints him differently, however, in altogether stronger colors. It is all to do with his uniqueness. How unique is he?

Before he had started his ministry of preaching and healing, when he was being baptized, a voice spoke from heaven *Thou art my Son, My beloved, on thee My favor rests.*

Again, *For God so loved the world that He gave His only begotten son that whosoever believeth on him shall not perish but have everlasting life.* That reference too was to Jesus.

Somehow, Christians believe that even in our own day the spiritual presence of Jesus can rest within a person and transform his behavior. He has seen that in Bahrein. There is a quality to mere living that he is somehow missing. He wants it for himself. Without it being present in others he would probably have been dead. Now he wants it in himself, desperately.

The Injil is not long, just a little longer that the Q'ran Sharif. By the time he comes through Torkham into the west end of the Khyber, two things have happened. He has read through the Injil from cover to cover half a dozen times, and he knows *whom he has believed and is persuaded that he is able to keep that which he has committed unto him against that day. 2 Timothy 1:12*

He's glad to be home. What a journey!

His mother and father are overjoyed. His fellow travelers had returned his suitcase and bedroll to them and reported him missing in Bahrein. It could have been he had absconded without documents into a wealthy Gulf economy; it could have been he was waylaid and murdered by thieves. No one knew. The parents are delighted that their son, the first hajji in their family, is safely back home. There is no avoiding the celebrations for his return. He is decked with the customary garlands of currency notes. People, even the friends of his youth, address him respectfully as "Haji Sah'b." He is a celebrity.

To Kalim it is all now hollow. He is waiting for things to settle down. He resumes his work with Radio Pakistan in Peshawar.

One weekend he is back home in the Pass. For a few hours there will be only his parents and himself. Now is the opportunity. They already know of the attack in Bahrein and that he has been cared for by a Christian family. They have observed the gentling of his character and gratefully credited the Hajj experience for changing their son so positively.

He asks them for permission to talk to them about something quite serious in his life. He takes them step-by-step through his long spiritual journey on the way home. His mother looks increasingly anguished. His father is hearing him out. His mother puts her hands to her ears. He tells them that he has no choice but to accept Jesus Christ as His Savior. He regrets the consequences for his family. He loves them very much. He is sorry to cause them pain. His mother runs from the room, wailing as though for the dead. His father, silent through it all, rises to his feet. "Better by far they had allowed you to die in Bahrein. You are no son of mine. My son is dead." He leaves the room without looking back.

That night, in the dim light, as Kalim sleeps, his mother comes to his room. She is armed with grim determination and a knitting needle. As he screams into wakefulness he hears the voice of his mother cursing him. If he will not read the Q'ran Sharif, there is no way he will read the Injil. She drives the knitting needle first into one eye and then the other.

His father and other members of the family come running and are confronted by what the mother has done. To his father he is already dead. The great gates swing open. His screams of pain have lapsed into groans. He is taken to the edge of the ravine that winds through the Khyber and his body pitched over into the deep night.

He knew not how long he lay on the floor of the ravine, a tumbled broken heap of flesh and bones with heart barely beating. A camel caravan of smugglers and carpet traders found him, discovered he was still alive, placed his body carefully across a camel's back and continued steadily towards Peshawar. They plied the man with water whenever his groans indicated his wakefulness.

Eventually, twenty-five miles and many hours later they leave him in Peshawar. At Dhabgharri Gate, in front of the Mission Hospital, they carefully place his body on the pavement. They bang on the gate to alert the watchman and then continue their slow journey towards Qissa Khawani Bazar. For a second time, Kalim's life has been saved by good Samaritans.

When Kalim was brought in, the duty doctor was alerted immediately. The eyes would have to wait until the more urgent other injuries had been patched, set and splinted, and the ribs strapped. Then the eyes. There was nothing there that could be done, that was obvious. The man would be permanently blind.

While Kalim was recovering, he told the staff his story. They knew exactly where he was from in the Khyber. Strangers at the gate began inquiring about his whereabouts and his welfare. Some when questioned claimed to be his relatives. They were told he was allowed no visitors.

It was time for Kalim to move on. But where? Where does a blind man go? A patient's relative was returning to Lahore after seeing to his mother's double cataract surgery. Yes, he would escort Kalim to Lahore and deliver him to a Roman Catholic Convent of Sisters with a note. Yes, no trouble at all.

Kalim now lives in Lahore. The nuns have been taking care of him, and he sells postcards at a pitch he has not far from the convent gates. The postcards, he shows me some, are Christian pictures of interest to Catholics. I ask him, for he still has many years of life ahead, whether there is anything that can be done about his eyes. He does not answer but quietly removes his dark glasses. There are just two empty eye sockets.

Strangely, very strangely, he does not appear to be angry.

SADIQ SHAMSHAD

Shamshad, the father of Sadiq, was the hostel boys' cook at the technical school. In order to try to deal with the boys' complaints of poor food in the hostels, the boys had been given the money for the food that was collected from them when they returned from holidays. It was their responsibility, through their own appointed food committee, to buy the food daily from the vegetable market according to season–atta flour for the bread and also meat twice a week on Thursdays and Sundays. They employed and paid the cook and, at the end of each term, accounted to the assembled hostel boys for their expenditures.

Meals were simple. Three meals a day. The evening meal was often reheated food from breakfast together with two pieces of bread. Lunch at 2 P.M. was lentils and vegetable curry and bread. Supper was a variation on lunch: vegetable curry, lentils and bread. For a change the boys had porridge on Sunday mornings and fresh vegetables like turnips when they were plentiful and inexpensive. Their drink was water.

The system didn't work well. Sometimes the boys on the hostel committee stole from the food money. None of the controls that were needed seemed to be working. Reluctantly we abandoned the fiction of the boys managing the hostel food arrangements. We also dismissed Shamshad for stealing. Not stealing food for his family from the boys cooking pot for we remembered *Muzzle not the ox that treadeth out the corn.* However, large quantities of uncooked food were also disappearing. There was further a growing unauthorized clientele for lunch. Various odd bodies regularly turned up to dine from Shamshad's largesse just before the boys arrived hungry from school.

Shamshad was a squatter, a Christian by birth, and he lived without paying rent in one of the Seminary servant quarters. He had two daughters who were nurses in the South of the country. They sent money home to help the parents and several younger sons. His oldest son was Sadiq, a ne'er-do-well in his late teens who had worked for me as a laborer on the building work, but who had been sacked for stealing.

Ahmed Din, the chief storekeeper and a fellow congregational elder, asked me one morning as I was leaving chapel whether I had heard about Sadiq Shamshad. "He's been struck blind, sir, by God!" Ahmed Din's further explanation was both confused and intriguing. I decided to find out for myself and turned towards the Seminary quarters.

His mother was a gentle, kindly and devout woman who was regularly part of Marie's women's missionary society meeting. She pointed me towards the room where Sadiq lay in bed propped up with pillows. His eyes were wide open, but he gave no hint of seeing me or registering my presence. I put up a finger to quiet his mother and tiptoed up to him. I waved my hand in front of his eyes. No flicker. I brought my hand down sharply in front of his eyes. Again, no flicker. Surely if he were shamming he would have given some sign of it. He had an awestruck look on his face, as though in the night he might just have gone outside and seen an angel with spread wings standing at the door. As far as he was concerned, he had.

I pulled up a chair beside the bed and asked Sadiq to tell me what had happened to him. He turned his head towards my voice–easily recognizable to him–salaam'd me and told an intriguing story. His mother broke in to supplement it with matters he forgot or passed by. I do not recollect fully the details of the dream that he told, but it went something like this.

Sadiq had been sleeping and when he awoke, he saw Jesus in the room with him. He knew immediately that it was Jesus. Jesus was clad in a white robe. He beckoned Sadiq to sit up, and Sadiq struggled out of bed to kneel before his night visitor. Jesus smiled at him and three times asked him the question, in Urdu, "Do you love me, Sadiq?" "Yes, Jesus, I love you." was his reply each time. Jesus pointed to the floor beside Sadiq. Lying there was a gold ring with a broad band. "Put it on my finger, Sadiq." Jesus stretched out his hand. The ring would not go on. "Try again, Sadiq." Again Sadiq tried and failed. "Try once more, Sadiq." The third time the ring slipped on the finger easily and loosely as though it had never been initially tight. He looked back up at Christ, still on his knees. "Sadiq, I am going to take away your sight so that you will know it was me who came to you, but Peter will come and give it back to you after a while."

Sadiq had burst into sobbing within his sleep. His convulsive weeping brought first his mother and then his father. He clung desperately to his mother, crying as though his heart would break. His father lit the oil lamp. As squatters, their electricity had been cut off. Sadiq told them of his dream. His father held up the oil lamp before his son's face. He peered into his son's eyes. The boy could feel the warmth of the lamp, but there was nothing to see of its light. When dawn came the effect was the same, darkness. Sadiq was blind.

What did this mean? Why had Sadiq lost his sight? Who was Peter? Was it Peter the Apostle? They knew many Peters. How many days, months, would they have to wait? What was the meaning of the dream?

Each day after chapel I went up to Shamshad's quarters. A doctor had come from the town. There was no doubt the boy could not see, but there seemed no physical reason why this should be so. He remained in bed showing little inclination to struggle to overcome the effects of his blindness. The boy's mother was busy every spare moment reading the Bible to her son. That seemed to be all he wanted.

One day, probably about a week later, Ahmed Din met me again after chapel. "Sadiq can see! It is done; Sadiq can see again."

This time it was Shamshad, the father, who explained what had happened. During his sleep that night, he had been told in a dream that Peter Langra would give his son back his sight, and he was to fetch him. Peter Langra was a rural pastor, a cripple who lived in a village miles away across the canal. Fortunately it was a moonlit night. It was after midnight that Shamshad set out. Soon he left the made up road and now it was over dirt tracks. When he arrived at Peter's village, he noticed to his surprise that there was still a light burning in the pastor's house.

He knocked, not too loudly at first, at the door to the courtyard. There was almost immediately movement within and then a shuffling sound as the pastor negotiated his way across the courtyard to open the gate. He looked out, peering to see who it was. "Are you Shamshad?" he asked. Startled at the question,

Shamshad replied, "Yes, I am Shamshad Masih, the cook from the technical school." "I have been waiting for you. Wait there a moment, I will be with you."

The pastor, to Shamshad's amazement, was fully dressed and obviously prepared to travel. He asked no questions but perched himself on the cross bar of Shamshad's bicycle for the bumpy miles back to the seminary. On the way he told the cook that he had been praying earlier that evening, and the Lord had told him that someone called Shamshad would be coming to fetch him later that night. He must go with him and do what he was directed to do when he arrived.

Mrs Shamshad soon had tea for them when they arrived as the first signs of dawn were beginning to streak the sky. They shared the experiences that had brought them together. For Peter, he was hearing the full story for the first time. It was clear what he had to do.

He prayed with Sadiq and then, balancing unsteadily behind the chair in which Sadiq sat, he placed his hands over Sadiq' eyes and said, "In the name of Jesus Christ the Lord, receive your sight. To God be the Glory. Amen."

Sadiq blinked his eyes, blinked them again, and then again. His expression was changing. From blankness and questioning, hope was spreading, jumping. It was becoming joy, just plain joy. Then, from his eyes, tears and tears and yet more tears flowed.

"I can see, I can see, I can see!"

When I came up after chapel, Sadiq was sitting on a chair, holding close to his heart his mother's Urdu Bible as though it were breath itself. He was glowing and radiant and gladly accepted my invitation to come to chapel next morning to tell what had happened to him.

It was a different Sadiq at chapel to the young man I had known. He was clad in his spotless best clothes, carefully ironed for him by his mother. He was shaven and smart, and again clutching his large Bible with both hands as though he would rather die than be separated from it. There was no acting, no histrionics, no pausing for effect. Quite simply and straightforwardly he told the story. The boys had known what he was like before. Well, this Sadiq they were seeing now was just not the same person. He had met Jesus. They needed to meet Jesus too. He had been blind. Did they have any idea what being blind really meant? If they hadn't given their hearts to Jesus they were blind too, even though they could see with their eyes. They should give their hearts to Jesus, and they would really begin to see in a way they had never seen before. It was all in the Bible. Glory be to God!

There was complete silence. You could have heard a pin drop. Something wonderful MUST have happened to Sadiq Shamshad, for they were certainly hearing and seeing someone completely different from the lad they had known before. They left the chapel for Bible class pensively. There was none of the hubbub of chatter that normally burst out as they went down the chapel steps.

I gave Sadiq a job as an assistant brick mason with the building crew and told him he would be free to take unpaid leave whenever he needed to go and share his story. He had many calls from various scattered village Christian communities those first few weeks and was frequently away from work.

About six weeks later I discovered Sadiq was stealing and selling bags of cement, and I sacked him once again. This marked the virtual end of his effective witness to the time when he was blind and Peter Langra healed him.

Mementos

*They never die who leave behind
Some wise and well remembered thing.
This lone race o'er, the brief span done,
They run renewed through fairer fields,
Childish in wonder, bright and fair.
Close behind them, hasting, pressing
Towards the great divide that marks
The highest point that man can rise
Climb the following wiser ones,
Bright in their youth, noble and sweet,
Chasing the far off shining Hope,
Singing on the way well marked
With signposts to the Infinite
That earlier travelers made.*

Epilogue

We have followed the fortunes and misfortunes of a dozen or so men and women whose stories have individually graced the life of northern India and surrounding countries in the past one and a half centuries. None of them is a well-known character, and most of them lie unmarked and forgotten.

There are many other stories of similar nature that continue down to the present day. Not for nothing is our past century notorious as the century of martyrs.

What is there in our religious attitudes that drives us towards a conservative fundamentalism that disallows so readily the rights of others to different views of God than those we ourselves possess and profess? Why are true liberalism and genuine tolerance dying at the turn of a century which at its beginning saw a flowering of liberal and tolerant ideas?

So Great a Cloud is of course not a balanced book. It happens merely to contain stories that have spoken to my heart in some way or other that I have wished to share. There are surely positive stories out of Hinduism and Islam that I could also have shared had I been aware of them. Christians have no corner on martyrs.

The real sadness is that the brutalities, the persecutions and pogroms, the punishments, the attrition of court cases and the occasional martyrdoms go on. Iniquitous laws at the national level designed to accommodate, quiet, and excuse political and religious bigotry and zealotry assist them.

We are no wiser than our fathers, frequently more extreme and dogmatic, and what hope have our children to be different than we are?

If things ever change, it will be because of the signposts to the infinite that people like Pipo, the weaver of Jhandran and Kanaya, the lambardar's son, and Esther and Zaid, the blind Afghan, erected ahead of us along the way.

Appendix

Urdu Dictionary

abbu	father
Amir	Afghan ruler
bazar	market
buzurg	elder
caravansarai	staging point for camel caravans
chapkan	long formal man's frockcoat
charpai	country bed strung with rope
chhappard	sewage pond on edge of village
chicks	flexible cloth-backed bamboo curtains
chimta	fire-tongs
D.C.	deputy commissioner
dharmsala	community guest house
dholi	palanquin
dholki	drum (large)
diva	clay oil lamp
durbar	meeting of eminences court
fakir	ascetic mendicant / holy man
guru	Hindu religious teacher
Hadis	Muslim traditions about Prophet Mohammed
Hajj	pilgrimage to Mecca
hajji	Mecca pilgrim
hukm	order, instruction
huqqa	smoker's bubble pipe
Iblis	devil, Satan
imam	Muslim religious leader
Injil	New Testament
Isa	Jesus
Isai	Christian
ji	"respected one"
kafir	unbeliever, infidel
kalma	Muslim creed
kutchery	courthouse, court
lambardar	headman of village

mahout	elephant keeper
maidan	parade ground
malikji	"respected tribal leader"
Masih	surname meaning "follower of the Messiah"
maulvi	Muslim priest
Meg	low Hindu caste of weavers
missahiba	single woman missionary
mujahideen	Afghan guerrillas
nullah	gully, creek, watercourse
padri	pastor
pandit	a learned Brahmin
Pathan	tribesman of the Northwest Frontier Province
pind	village
pir	Muslim holy man / religious leader
pleader	legal advocate
puggree (cloth)	turban
Pushtu	language of Pathan tribesmen
pukka	correct, first class, well-built
Punjab	land of the five rivers
qazi	Muslim judge, secular and religious
Q'ran	The Holy Koran, Quran
Raj	British rule in India
raja, rani, nawab	native rulers
sadhu	Hindu or Christian holy man
sah'b, sahib	white man
sah'b logue	the white people
Saiyad	descendant of Mohammed
salaam, salaamji	greeting of peace
tabla	drum (small)
thik hai	'OK', fair enough
Torah	books of Moses (Pentateuch)
Urdu	principal language of Pakistan
Wazir	Minister, Prime Minister
Yisu	Jesus
Zaburs	Psalms

Contact Kenneth Old
or order more copies of this book at

TATE PUBLISHING, LLC

127 East Trade Center Terrace
Mustang, OK 73064

888.361.9473

www.tatepublishing.com